PULSE OF THE FOREST

A guide to the vitality and variety
of life in our broadleaf woodlands

by James P. Jackson

Photography by the author

PULSE OF THE FOREST

A guide to the vitality and variety
of life in our broadleaf woodlands

Photography by the author

To Charlene,
Keith and Glenn

CONTENTS

FOREWORD

The groves may have been God's first temples, as William Cullen Bryant asserted in his *Forest Hymn,* but early Americans seem to have been more fearful than reverent of the great arboreal landscape that swept across so much of the land these venturesome Europeans wanted to reduce to tamed wealth.

Trees and groves were sacred to early Greeks, and to Romans who inherited (and cheapened) their religious thought, but Mediterranean islands are bare now and so is most of Italy...wind-scoured, rain-gullied. And where are those holy cedars of Lebanon that supplied pillars for the Temple?

It may be best that James P. Jackson doesn't take a theological view within these pages about a deciduous forest. He takes about every other view, though: soil and sun, rocks and rain, weevils and wildlife, moths and microorganisms. And man, of course; man as hunter, fisher, miner, logger, student, wanderer or poet. And photographer, for Jim Jackson aimed his cameras at some commonplace items that were thereby transmuted to gold.

It would be pleasant but false to say I predicted this book a quarter century ago on first meeting Jim as he became an education advisor with the Missouri Conservation Commission, that revolutionary wildlife-forestry agency whose chief founder more than 40 years ago was E. Sydney Stephens. Mr. Stephens, first and decade-long chairman of the Commission, announced and enforced his conservation philosophy in these words: "All life begins with the soil. Let us, then, begin *our* work with the soil."

Young Jackson fit squarely into that simple-complex precept; as an agency employee and, later, as a teacher, he always began at the beginning.

A major disadvantage of becoming old is that you keep hearing what you heard before (and keep writing what you've written before). But a pleasure of longevity is the chance to watch young idealists become mature, thoughtful forces shaping slow public understanding of resources and our environment. Jim became one of those forces, and this book proves it. He isn't trying to prove anything, though—just to demonstrate something important: hardwoods.

He wants to demonstrate it to those U. S. citizens who massively misunderstand the life processes that support us. He treats the trees that combine into a forest as It, not Them, for here species interest him less than the integration of living things that we call, inelegantly, eco-system. Jim wants us to see it whole, this community we name a forest, to peer into its mold beneath fallen leaves and to view the sweep of it.

So he touches upon almost everything connected with a wide stand of hardwood trees, without preconceived notions of easy moralism. As biologist or botanist he speculates upon clear cutting, aesthetics and recreation while avoiding the ideologies that confuse timber management and public policy. He defines, by inference, wise use of wooded areas whether owned publicly, commercially or by smallholders. Good and Evil are frequently matters of degree: controlled fires can be good for a forest, uncontrolled deer can be bad for a forest. Timber should be harvested, but methods should fit topography, wild animals, a sense of beauty, a belief in the future of forests and wild creatures and human beings. Positivists beware.

Any intelligent readers will learn a great deal about forests that shed their leaves, about the natural (and unnatural) foes of trees, about wood for workmen and solace for souls within shaded landscapes. They will learn about the sources of rivers —and even a certain reverence that has little to do with ritual but perhaps much to do with the poetizing of William Cullen Bryant. There may be nothing supernatural in forests, but there *is* something so deeply natural that we may have lost it in artificial living.

What we should all learn is here, too: how to use well our great renewable resource, the forests of the United States.

Dan Saults, President
Outdoor Writers Association of
America, 1979–80

INTRODUCTION

It has many times been my pleasure to lead youngsters on instructive walks in the woods. My goals on such outings have always been to teach the senses to observe and to instill an appreciation for the natural world. If I can get each individual to notice just a few living things and find pleasure in their uniqueness, then I feel my efforts rewarded. But it can also be a learning experience for me.

Interpreting the reactions of my young recruits is sometimes a challenge. Some are wide-eyed with wonder and make the work pleasurable: "Look at the size of that huge tree!" Others are vaguely fearful of the unfamiliar: "Can that toad really give me warts?" But there are always a few who seem totally indifferent—no questions, no comments, blank expressions on their faces. Those who act bored are of more concern to me than the overinquisitive. I judge that certain facets of their upbringing have taught them to believe that the natural world is neither necessary nor worth their attention. Theirs is a common affliction in our highly urbanized, highly industrialized society; such attitudes are unfortunate for and even dangerous to the future inhabitants of this green earth.

Anything is worthwhile that serves to arouse our curiosity in the natural world and enables us to appreciate the necessary role it plays in our lives. My efforts in this book, within the scope of these limited goals, are focused on the deciduous forests of the eastern United States.

When Europeans first settled along our shores, most primeval land east of the Mississippi River was in unbroken deciduous forest; the only exceptions were bands of coniferous woodlands along today's northern tier of states and along the southern coasts, plus limited areas of prairie in Illinois, Indiana, and southern Wisconsin. Today more than half of that vast, unbroken forest land has been eliminated by our agriculture, highways, cities, and towns. Of what remains, nearly three-fourths is in small privately owned woodlots that are generally not well managed for perpetuation. And yet well over half of our population must consider deciduous woodland as the most accessible natural landscape—the most familiar realm in which to seek kinship with nature.

But it is not all that familiar, as witness my own experiences in leading youngsters into the woods. Too many American adults, as reflected in their children, have yet to outgrow what is sometimes referred to as the Little Red Riding Hood complex: to them the woods are still inhabited by wolves and loathsome creatures of imagination. Some who grew up close to the wilds are no less troubled in this respect than are the true urbanites. Some people can hardly see beyond the super-market and the factory; their indifference to the natural world is transmitted to their children. Even among the many people who seek actively to enjoy the woods, there are those who feel inadequate if they cannot learn to name each tree, shrub, wildflower, and animal observed; unfamiliar forms, regardless of their inherent beauty or uniqueness, are seldom appreciated as they should be. But there are really no good reasons for either the timid or the uninformed to avoid the woods.

The hazards of exploring a woodland trail are considerably less than those of walking city streets, and trying to know every resident of either community would be impossible. What is far more important is trying to understand and appreciate living relationships—in short, *ecology*. Thus this book seeks to explore some vital interactions among plants and animals that make up the complex fabric of the deciduous forest. It also examines how man relates to it—how we sometimes abuse it by greed or ignorance, how we can preserve its recreation potentials, and how we must protect what remains before the grinding wheels of progress roll over it and destroy it.

Since my work on this book encompassed the illustrating as well as the writing, I feel a need to describe my methods of woodland photography. With few exceptions the photos were taken with a high-quality 35 mm. camera, one adapted for a variety of interchangeable lenses. I refrain from naming the particular brand simply because there are others equally as good, and equally expensive. To me the important requirements—in addition to quality—are versatility with a minimum of bulk and weight.

The three lenses I use most frequently have the following focal lengths: 35 mm. (wide-angle), 55 mm. macro (normal but specially adapted for close ups), and 300 mm. (medium telephoto). A variety of accessories such as filters, flash, tripod, and cable release are also carried afield.

Every type of photography offers challenges. A prime consideration in woodlands is the contrasting nature of available light; scenery shadowed by trees and yet dappled with sunlight can make it extremely difficult to get a proper exposure. It is often easier to shoot woodland scenes on hazy or completely overcast days; this, of course, demands time exposures and the steadiness provided by the use of a tripod and cable release.

Flash is hardly effective beyond 20 feet and so is useless for any kind of scenery. Available-light close-ups of wildflowers are possible in spring, before trees leaf out, but they are easily blurred by motion from the slightest breezes; flash is often useful in such situations. Because animals move more quickly and unpredictably than wind-blown plants, they offer many photo challenges. Blinds are necessary for hiding from birds, and flash is required to stop the action of small animals. The techniques in either case are much too involved for me to describe in these brief introductory comments. However, I feel obliged to offer one piece of advice to potential nature photographers. If you need to stage a setting for any small, captured creature—a procedure often necessary—make certain that you know the behavior and habitat preference of the species well enough to guarantee a miniature scene that is truly authentic. The camera may shoot reasonably clear photos for the nature faker, but he is certain to render a bad image of himself among those who know better.

Preparation of this book has led the author into many pathways of woodland pleasure and enlightenment, and there are many people who have helped guide my way. It would be impossible to name them all. Included are teachers from childhood days, summer camp counselors, and excellent amateur naturalists. Then there are the professionals: faculty members of the University of Missouri School of Forestry, Fisheries and Wildlife, plus staff personnel of the Missouri Department of Conservation. All of them, by design or accident, have imbued me with enthusiasm for the natural world in ways that are incurable. I thank every one of them. I also hope that my efforts can do the same for others. □

James P. Jackson
Marthasville, Missouri
Summer of 1980

THE FOREST COMMUNITY

Most people appreciate the forest closest to home, the one most familiar to them. But for those who know many types, who will deny the superior beauty of temperate, deciduous forests? They are blessed with great diversity, but better yet, they are fascinating for their changes through four seasons; this, more than anything else, is their distinction.

Thus the forest to be described here can probably be better recognized by its four seasons than by its particular trees. A person may not know one tree from another but will have a good mental image of the carpet of lovely wildflowers that blossom in spring before leaves emerge on the trees. Also memorable are the languid days of summer, a time when birds and mammals produce their adorable youngsters. And who has not enjoyed, even through photos, the colorful days of autumn as contrasted to the winter of stark, naked trees awaiting another spring? Most people can at least recognize a deciduous forest when they see one.

But to realize just how a forest is a community of great complexity and diversity is another matter. A few people may view it as just a bunch of trees, or an alien place with threatening creatures, or as real estate to be bought and sold for whatever the market will allow. These people are blind to important values.

Basic levels of life and relationships are somewhat similar in all natural communities, yet maybe they are easier to see and understand in a deciduous forest. First, of course, are the dominant trees. They cover the forest like a great overlapping umbrella, one that shades out sunlight below while at the same time capturing it as the main source of energy for the entire forest. The energy is trapped in the leaves, billions of them, to manufacture food through photosynthesis for the trees and whatever feeds on them, whether directly or indirectly. Some of the sun's energy is also trapped by early spring wildflowers and later on by other low plants efficient enough to use the dim light that penetrates the forest umbrella.

There are, in effect, four levels of food producers in a deciduous forest. First is the canopy, the umbrella of foliage which is maintained by dominant trees: the oaks, hickories, ashes, maples, beech, black walnut, tulip poplar, and whatever additional species might grace particular woods. Below that is an understory of lesser trees that can tolerate shade from above; among the better-known of these are flowering dogwood, buckeye, ironwood, and redbud. Then there are the shrubs, usually less than head high, which grow in dense clumps where competition from dominant trees is not too great. And finally, emerging from the carpet of fallen leaves and other litter, there are wildflowers and other lowly plants. Many find their place in the sun during early spring and then, after trees leaf out, begin dying back until another year. Ferns, however, are well-adapted to poor light conditions and will stay green all summer if there is enough moisture.

All of the plants mentioned, in whatever levels, help to guarantee both shelter and nutrition for animals of the forest. They are the first part of all food chains. They include leaves that fatten caterpillars to feed the songbirds, wood eaten by beetles that are pried out of trees by woodpeckers, berries nibbled by white-footed mice preyed upon by foxes, and nuts

White-footed mouse peering out of its hiding place in a fallen log

Whitetail- deer fawn about one week old

gnawed by squirrels which may in turn be snatched out of trees by soaring hawks. Many food chains are longer, but they come in endless variety. Green plant to vegetarian to predator —it is the same system that moves food and energy through all natural communities.

And there are other relationships, some of them just as important but seldom appreciated. Parasitism is one of them. Occasionally in our deciduous forests, due perhaps to mild winters, or a shortage of specific predators, or introduction of foreign species, certain moths do great damage to tree foliage. Their caterpillars chew one leaf after another—tons of them in a forest—and may completely defoliate the green canopy. The imported gypsy moth is one of the worst defoliators, but there are native species that occasionally do the same thing. Yet the native species are often controlled by native parasites, especially the tiny braconid wasps which deposit their eggs either in eggs of moths or in newly hatched caterpillars. When the moths multiply to large populations, the pinhead-size braconids begin to muster increasing numbers. The wasps' populations at first lag behind, but in time they completely overtake the defoliaters and collapse their numbers. As an example, between 1968 and 1971 the oak forests of Missouri suffered increasing defoliation by a previously uncommon insect known as the variable oakleaf caterpillar. After defoliation of millions of acres of forestland in Missouri during late summer of 1971, these caterpillars could hardly be found the following year; braconids wiped them out.

This has not been the case, of course, where gypsy moths have done severe damage in the northeastern states. But neither is this imported species subject to the checks and balances that American deciduous forests have adapted with their own species over thousands of years.

Another type of relationship not often appreciated is symbiosis, also known as mutualism. This is where one species of living thing is adapted to mutual partnership with another in which both parties benefit in some way. A well-known example, studied in all high school and college biology classes, is that of lichens which grow on rocks and tree trunks. A tangle of fungus threads absorbs moisture and minerals from the surface it lives on, or from the air, and microscopic algae living in the tangle do the photosynthesizing which provides food for both. Another example, known as mycorrhiza, involves partnership between fungi and the tiny rootlets of forest trees upon which they live; the process is not completely understood, but it is known that the trees,

A nest of baby robins in a wild black cherry tree

Great-spangled fritillary on a thistle

A male red-bellied woodpecker, typical of deciduous forests

The five-lined or blue-tailed skink, guarding her eggs

particularly younger ones, grow much better roots with the fungi attached. Then there is the classic example of squirrels burying nuts and acorns, which otherwise have little chance to germinate, in mineral soil through a thick carpet of forest litter; those not later found by the squirrels have a good chance to grow into trees. The squirrels and trees help each other.

Among the most important relationships for a healthy forest community are those involving decomposers. Autumn's fallen leaves, dead trees, and dead animals—all need to be recycled to maintain the fertility of the forest. To help in this there are many creatures, from leaf mold to termites to scavengers that feed on dead carcasses. Even the vulture which soars on set wings over the forest canopy, or rests high on a dead snag, is part of this relationship; the waste from his meal of carrion falls and, in its special way, enriches a bit of forest soil.

The total number of species playing their specific roles in a deciduous forest is most important. The more the better; this is a point often overlooked by people who question the value of this or that animal. Consider an example. If the little white-footed mouse so common to deciduous forests could reproduce at its maximum potential, it would literally overrun its environment. A typical pair averages four mice per litter, and there are usually two litters in spring plus one or two more in autumn; spring-born litters often mature in time to mate and produce their own offspring before winter. If all survived, each and every pair could increase to more than 30 in a year. Fortunately, of course, there are foxes, hawks, owls, and snakes to eat their share of mice; diseases, internal parasites, floods, and the trials of winter will also reduce the numbers. But just imagine what would happen if there was just one mouse predator in the forest and it happened to suffer an epidemic disease. Other types of mortality would not be able to control the prolific white-foot. Thus diversity serves as a cushion against disaster.

The variable oakleaf caterpillar and other potential defoliators of forest trees seldom have population explosions—not necessarily because of the braconid wasp, but likely because they are normally controlled by a whole variety of enemies. We may not appreciate all of them, but, hidden as they might be to us, they are probably there. The founding fathers of the United States devised many checks and balances for our democratic form of government; yet many people never realize that checks and balances are also important to a forest community. A case in point is the careless, indiscriminate use of pesticides. Insect poisons can too easily wipe out beneficial

Immature great horned owl in an oak tree

insects along with the target species. Destroying whole food chains is no way to maintain the health of any natural community. There are hidden dangers in all kinds of monoculture.

Plants and animals everywhere develop their relationships through evolution. Creatures unsuited to the deciduous forest, and temporary imbalances of populations, all have gradually been worked out over many centuries. Climate has been an important factor in the process; few natural communities offer such contrasts of seasonal heat and cold, moisture and dryness, as the deciduous forests. Temperatures may be subarctic for a time in January and equatorial in July. Though precipitation is usually abundant, severe drought conditions are not a rarity. Thus the same forces which make for four distinct seasons also have adapted plants and animals to climatic extremes.

One other natural force occasionally influences and shapes a deciduous forest. It is fire. It can be highly destructive or sometimes beneficial, depending on its timing and other factors. A blaze fanned by hot winds during extreme drought, especially after years of litter buildup on the forest floor, can be disastrous. It may not be so terrible as to burn in the forest crown, as it would in a coniferous forest, but it can wipe out young trees and damage larger ones by causing permanent fire scars at the base of their trunks. Such a fire will also reduce wildlife populations for several years. But an early spring fire, especially when underpinnings of the forest floor are damp and litter is not too abundant, can be beneficial. It can prevent undue buildup of litter and will reduce low-growing plants which compete with seedling trees; oaks often sprout with increased vigor from roots after such fires. Today, where man has a large measure of control, fire can be a valuable management tool in a forest, but it should be used only by trained foresters.

What applies to man's use of fire is currently less of a problem than how the harvest of trees for wood products is managed. There is much debate over clearcutting versus selective logging of trees. The first method is cheaper to manage and allows the start of a completely new crop of trees after cutting; it is also unsightly and, in large patches, can cause severe erosion. The selective method is less economical but preserves the beauty of a forest and its attractiveness for all sorts of recreation. Another activity often debated is whether or not to remove trees that are worthless for wood products; they may compete with the commercial types but, on the other hand, often provide food and denning places for wildlife. In summary, an undisturbed forest is a place of beauty that usually

The same fallen log shown in spring, summer, autumn, and winter

maintains a dynamic balance; yet if it has commercial value, it will always be subjected to conflicting demands.

The worst thing that can happen to a deciduous forest is complete removal from the landscape. This means clearing for farms, highways, and all forms of urban sprawl. It is true that much of the original forest once covering the eastern United States is now cleared for these other uses; very little of it will ever revert to forest. But nearly all of what remains should be preserved intact. The deciduous forest as a natural community is too valuable in its varied uses for man to do otherwise. Most importantly, perhaps, it is a part of man's community also. □

FRATERNITIES

From the Atlantic Ocean west to the Great Plains, and from the Gulf Coast to the Great lakes, deciduous forest covers a wide range of soil types and climatic conditions. Most of the tree species, however, have their own limited ranges of tolerance. The beech is as alien to an Ozark ridge as the bur oak is to an Appalachian slope or the yellow buckeye is to a Mississippi River floodplain. Yet all three of these species, as well as over 100 others, are part of the tapestry of trees that covers the eastern United States. Only a few species—the American elm is a notable example—range throughout the entire deciduous-forest region.

Wherever they thrive, native trees seem as choosy about their neighbors as they are about soil and climate. They tend

13

to grow in predictable associations which, when long-established, are referred to as climax forests. And since these associations show their best development where they are undisturbed by human influences, the ones I have chosen to describe for this chapter are from virgin tracts. They represent parcels of primeval America that are as fascinating as they are rare.

A good place to begin is where the most diverse associations and the largest trees can be found. This—the ancestral birthplace for most deciduous trees—is in the southern Appalachians, in the general area of Great Smoky Mountains National Park.

Within this area, an outstanding example is Joyce Kilmer Memorial Forest, in North Carolina's Nantahala National Forest. Its nearly 4,000 acres were dedicated for preservation in 1936, to immortalize the author of the poem *Trees.* The tract slopes upward along both sides of Little Santeetlah Creek and is well shielded from hot, westerly winds of summer and icy blasts of winter. Elevation differences of more than 2,000 feet allow for local variations within the already diverse tree association.

The lowest, most sheltered part of this forest harbors some of the largest deciduous trees anywhere: tulip poplars fully six feet in diameter and 150 feet tall. Associated with them are large specimens of beech, basswood, yellow buckeye, several species of oak, and many lesser trees. In places they brood over sickly sprouts of chestnuts, reminding us of how this magnificent tree, before advent of the chestnut blight, once shared in dominating the forest. Among the deciduous species, Joyce Kilmer Forest also supports two evergreens, white pine and eastern hemlock; these grow to large size in spite of being nearly at the southern extremity of their natural range.

Here is an association of trees so varied that it cannot be named for its dominant species, as is often done—there are simply too many. Thus it is often referred to as mixed mesophytic, the latter word implying that it is blessed with more than ample precipitation but also has good drainage.

Where equally generous precipitation combines with poor drainage, as along the floodplains of major rivers, the forest is better referred to as hydrophytic. Most such places—except for swamps nearly impossible to drain—have long ago been cleared for agriculture. There are nevertheless a few virgin tracts still in existence.

One of the finest was nearly logged off in 1963. Miss Laura Beall had always wanted her 300 acres of primeval forest, adjoining the west bank of the Wabash River in Illinois, to be

The oak-hickory association is common. This example is in eastern Missouri

preserved. But she made no arrangements for this in her will. After she died, in 1961, her heirs sold the property to a wealthy farmer, who soon let it be known that he would have it logged off and cleared for agriculture. Conservationists quickly rallied and persuaded the state to use its power of eminent domain. In an unusual court case, 15 people testified in behalf of preservation and against the farmer. In winning its judgment, the state of Illinois had to pay the man a handsome price, but Laura Beall's original wish was ultimately honored—the virgin tract is now part of a state park.

Beall Woods, though it includes some upland, is best known as a floodplain forest. Among its dominant trees are giant sweetgums, swamp white oaks, bur oaks, pin oaks, pecans, sycamores, and silver maples. It also boasts the largest Shumard oaks anywhere, including the national champion, which is more than 16 feet in circumference and over 100 feet tall.

For champion-size deciduous trees, however, no place can rival Big Oak Tree State Park, an isolated preserve on the Mississippi floodplain of Missouri's bootheel. Completely surrounded by a sea of intensively cultivated corn, cotton, and soybean fields, it is an island remnant of what was once a vast forest of giants.

The park's 80 acres of virgin timber were set aside primarily to protect the largest bur, or mossycup, oak in existence. This champion, when it died in 1954, boasted a circumference of more than 21 feet and a height of 143 feet and had lived 334 years. Since its passing, the remnant forest has acquired fame as the home of nine other national-champion trees. Included are such outstanding specimens as a shellbark hickory nearly 13 feet in circumference, a persimmon 131 feet tall, and a swamp chestnut oak—currently the largest tree in the park—with a height of 142 feet and a circumference of almost 21 feet.

One feature shared by many trees growing in seasonally flooded areas is the tendency to develop buttressed, or flaring, bases. This may serve to aid in supporting the massive weight of their crowns and trunks in alluvial soil that is kept loose by saturation with water. The large Shumard oaks of Beall Woods and many species in Big Oak Tree State Park exhibit this feature.

But the most exaggerated buttresses are typically found on two species adapted to growing in standing water most of the time; these are the deciduous-needled cypress and the water tupelo. They represent the extremes in hydrophytic trees. The association that includes cypress and tupelo is still common in the southern states, mainly because large swamps tend to resist all attempts to drain them for agriculture. Extensive

This towering American elm in Big Oak Tree State Park, Missouri, chooses impressive neighbors—nine national champions

stands of these trees are to be found in such swamps as the Great Dismal, Okefenokee, and the Everglades—all in the southeastern states—and at Reelfoot Lake in western Tennessee.

One additional type of floodplain forest merits attention. That is the pioneer growth of trees that invades new river islands and those lands created by shifting of river channels within the broader spans of their valleys. Here is found a sequence that begins with willows, especially on sandbars, followed by fast-growing species such as silver maple, boxelder, sycamore, and cottonwood.

In certain locations, cottonwood grows to dominate all the others. Along the lower Mississippi River, it develops into groves more than 100 feet tall, with some individuals increasing their diameter at the rate of nearly two inches per year. Yet such stands are only temporary. If left undisturbed, the pioneer floodplain trees are ultimately replaced by the kinds of climax associations typical of Beall Woods and Big Oak Tree State Park.

To see the opposite of floodplain forests—the xerophytic types of drier areas—you need to visit the western edge of the forest region. From the drier ridges of southwest Missouri all the way to central Texas, a common association includes post oak and blackjack oak, neither one growing taller than about 60 feet at maturity. On some soil types, especially farther north, another species typical of the prairie frontier is the bur oak; it grows even as far west as the Black Hills of South Dakota.

Wherever they persist, these trees are adapted to compete with the grasses of a drier climate. They may be viewed either as the front line of an advancing forest or as the rearguard of one in retreat from dryness, prairie fires, or encroaching agriculture.

Of all tree associations west of the Appalachians, the most extensive is oak-hickory forest. It ranges from central Tennessee westward across northern Arkansas into a corner of Oklahoma, turning sharply northward to southeastern Nebraska, then going eastward all the way into southern Michigan; from there it angles southward back to Tennessee, thus forming a broad oval. Among its best-known trees are red and white oak, shagbark and mockernut hickory, white ash, basswood, and black walnut. Typical shade-tolerant understory trees include flowering dogwood, ironwood, redbud, and Ohio buckeye.

Perhaps the best example of oak-hickory forest remaining in its virgin state is found in east-central Missouri. Wegener Woods, some 40 acres in size, has been owned by the same

The author examines a large black walnut tree in Cox's Woods, a virgin tract in Indiana

family, one generation after another, since 1852. Though it harbors all species mentioned above, its most abundant is the white oak, represented by many fine specimens over 200 years old. Virgin tracts located in Indiana and Ohio are comparable but have some differences. They are not truly oak-hickory but tend to blend into the beech-maple association that adjoins it to the northeast.

Beech-maple forest, typical of cooler and more humid climates, extends all the way to the coniferous forests of the Great Lakes region and into New England. Like many deciduous types, this fraternity supports other species. It is, however, best recognized by two constants: American beech and sugar maple. These two must compete with oaks and hickories in Indiana; in New England they are crowded by white pine and hemlock. Even so, as with all associations, there can be some surprises.

This is amply illustrated at Turkey Run State Park in west-central Indiana. There you can find, on a few dry ridges, an oak-hickory forest similar to that of the Missouri Ozarks. You can also find, on certain nearby slopes, virgin beech-maple forest. And most surprising of all, you can even approach hemlock trees that grow precariously on the rims of narrow, cool canyons chilled on even the hottest summer days by spring-fed streams below. The hemlocks persist there, 200 miles from their accustomed range, as relics of a forest that retreated northward after the last ice age.

The beech-maple forest and its variations take us back full circle to the Appalachians, from whence all deciduous trees are believed to have evolved long before the Ice Age. After the continental glaciers pushed all forest types southward, they finally retreated and permitted forest to advance northward again. Then the deciduous types diversified and left us with the present associations which, once again, are being altered or totally destroyed—this time by the pressures of modern civilization.

The virgin remnants of deciduous forest associations, now so few and widely scattered, have thus become much more valuable than the sum of all their individual trees.

The places I have described are valuable first of all as irreplaceable museum pieces of primeval America. In an age when the natural world is constantly taking a beating, they are uniquely beautiful. Secondly, they are references, or benchmarks, for the various natural associations of trees; unfortunately in this respect, not all existing types are thus represented and preserved. Finally, virgin tracts serve as valuable

Virgin floodplain forest grows—and dies—in Beall Woods, Illinois

Cypress rise from the still water of swampy Reelfoot Lake, Tennessee

21

outdoor laboratories for studying long-term changes in forest communities. One example involves the Wegener Woods tract in Missouri.

In spite of its many old-growth white oaks, Wegener Woods has not exhibited any reproduction of this species for at least three decades. Instead, there has been replacement of dying oaks by sugar maples, which are scarcely represented among the older trees of the tract. A likely reason for this, in the opinion of forest ecologists, is that fire has not occurred in the tract for at least 40 years. Long-term protection from ground fires apparently tends to discourage white-oak reproduction. It also results in buildup of humus, which improves water-holding capacity of the soil; this in turn encourages reproduction and growth of sugar maple, a species more demanding of water than the oaks.

Stating it another way, there is some evidence from Wegener Woods that occasional ground fires may be needed to perpetuate a true oak-hickory forest. Whether this is correct or not, compiling similar evidence would be impossible in a woodland subjected to various human disturbances.

A few choice virgin tracts, fortunately, are either owned or held in trust by universities and studied on a continuing basis. One of the best-known is the William L. Hutcheson Memorial Forest, a tract of 60 acres in New Jersey. It has for many years been used as a prime research area by Rutgers University.

In the final analysis, though, an observer does not have to visit a primeval forest to learn how tree associations develop. They are constantly doing so wherever we give them a chance by practicing good forestry. The best feature of all deciduous forests is that they are renewable. □

HOW DOES A FOREST GROW?

A deciduous forest holds many values for man, but, in the long run, one always seems more important than all others. How many board-feet of wood can it grow in how many years?

This commercial viewpoint, so important to the woodland owner who must pay taxes and who desires an income, cannot be taken lightly. Yet the very patterns of growth—miracles by which trees convert air, water, and soil minerals into towering pillars of wood—are also important. They determine the abundance, health, and welfare of all forest inhabitants, animal as well as vegetable. They are worth observing and understanding.

Plants do not grow in the same way as animals. Most animals

25

grow only so much and then, after reaching maturity, get no larger. There are some exceptions, such as fishes and reptiles, which never completely stop growing; but their lives are rather short. A tree, on the other hand, grows as long as it has the spark of life; even when old and diseased, it endures year after year while dying branch by branch.

Another difference between plant and animal growth is on the microscopic level—that is, in how their cells develop. Animals produce cells, either for growth or repair, in all parts of their bodies. Such cells specialize immediately into skin, muscle, bone, and other tissues as they are formed by division of other cells. Plants follow a different pattern: they produce new cells in restricted areas only, and all are the same at first; they specialize later.

The areas of cell production in plants, known as meristems, are basically three in number. One is just behind root tips, the second is in growing shoots of upward and outward growth, and the third is a paper-thin cambium layer between the bark and the inner parts of woody plants. Cells divide and redivide within each meristem. Later they become inflated with life's juices, stiffen in capsules of cellulose, then specialize into leaves, stems, roots, and reproductive parts.

In trees there is a fourth meristem outside of the inner bark. It is the cork cambium and produces only one type of cell: outer bark. The main cambium, however, produces cells that develop into inner bark on one side and wood on the other. Some of the inner bark cells then specialize into phloem tubes that transport sap downward, while some of the wood cells become xylem tubes to haul sap upward in the tree.

These details of growth, when compared to those of animals, tell us that the growing part of a tree is on the outside. It is a living glove whose fingers lengthen as roots and twigs get longer, and expands as branches and the trunk grow in diameter. The interior, meanwhile, dies from the center outward; after its early years, the tree becomes a living shell surrounding dead heartwood.

Annual rings of growth, always visible in sanded and stained cross-sections of wood, result from inward additions by the cambium. Their early spring cells are larger and make softer wood than those produced in summer; they are also lighter in color. The darker, thinner line that separates one annual ring from the next is therefore referred to as summer wood. Although the hardening of wood is a gradual process as cellulose thickens the cell walls, it remains surprisingly porous as long as sap rises through its xylem tubes. A delicate instru-

Year-old white oak seedlings

Dendrometer will indicate slight swelling when soil moisture is abundant, shrinking when it is scarce

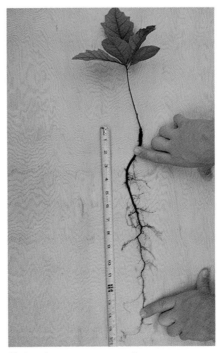

Extensive taproot sustains a one-year-old white oak seedling

Missouri forester Carl Robine inspects a mature white oak

Cross-section of white oak showing bark, sapwood, heartwood, annual growth rings, and rays

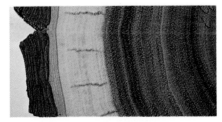

Cross-section of black walnut showing bark, sapwood, and the dark, valuable heartwood

ment known as a dendrometer, when wrapped tightly around the trunk, will indicate even slight swelling when soil moisture is abundant, and slight shrinking when it is scarce.

In the cross-section of a tree, as it matures, there is an indistinct line of changing color where cellular tubes are becoming clogged and the wood is dying. This line between living sap-wood and dead heartwood shows up quite clearly in some trees. In the black walnut, for example, the darker heartwood is of much greater commercial value than the light-colored sapwood.

In a few trees, such as the white oak, other lines show up in a cross-section of wood. These radiate outward, like spokes on a wheel, and are called rays. They are the product of specialization that creates plates of water-impervious cells; they are the reason white oak wood is so valuable in the manufacture of liquid-tight cooperage, or barrels.

Earlier I stated that a tree never stops growing as long as it has the spark of life. This applies only to growth in diameter. Trees that fulfill a complete normal lifespan will stop growing in height long before they begin to die. This is probably due to inherent limits in upward efficiency of the xylem tubes that haul sap up to their crowns. Here we should remind ourselves that tree sap rises without benefit of a pumping heart and other moving parts such as valves to prevent backflow. Sap is lifted by means of subtle forces acting on unbroken columns of liquid within tubes of very small diameter. One force is capillary action, and the other is upward pull of moisture—as though through a soda straw—while water is being lost to the atmosphere from thousands of tiny pores under each green leaf. The combined effect is sometimes referred to as transpiration pull.

The xylem tubes of California's coast redwoods permit a rise of sap to well over 300 feet. The highest that deciduous trees can grow is about half that; the uppermost movement of their sap is limited, no doubt, by inherent cell structure and by the seasonal flow as these trees go dormant in winter. Be that as it may, each species apparently has a maximum ceiling of growth.

Patterns of growth in various trees are distinctive and of great importance to the science of forestry. Other factors being equal, the faster a tree grows, generally the softer its wood and the shorter its life. Inheritance has some influence, but so do environmental conditions where the tree grows. Cotton-woods are among the fastest-growing, especially in the lower Mississippi River Valley; I have seen specimens 100 feet tall

Leader of a white oak, receiving sun in a clearing, begins to shoot up

and 30 inches in diameter when less than 30 years old. Near the opposite extreme are post oaks growing on Ozark ridges; I have seen specimens only six inches in diameter and yet over 100 years of age.

Soil type, climate, and moisture conditions are each important in determining what kind of trees will grow in a particular forest. Within these limits, however, nothing is more vital than a tree's ability to grow in available light. Foresters refer to this factor as tolerance to shade. Some deciduous species, such as the cottonwood, cannot survive under shade of other trees; they are considered intolerant. Sugar maple and beech, on the other hand, are among the most shade tolerant. Other species, including most of the oaks, show tolerance in early years but gradually lose it and therefore must have some direct sunlight in order to mature.

The white oak has an interesting growth pattern when over-shadowed by mature trees; one virtue of this valuable, long-lived species is its enduring patience. Yet oddly enough, it begins life as though it is terribly impatient. Its fall-ripening acorns, instead of waiting for spring to germinate, do so imme-diately after falling to the ground in autumn. The majority—even if not eaten by squirrels, deer, wild turkeys, wood-peckers, jays, and acorn weevils—may freeze before securing roots into mineral soil. Squirrels bury many and later dig them up with the guidance of their keen noses; yet a certain number are never retrieved. The spring after a good acorn year often finds tiny white oak seedlings cropping up all over the forest floor. Then for years they barely survive under shade of mature trees.

Seedling white oaks may grow only an inch or two per year, and be nibbled away by animals and scorched by ground fires; yet their patient, sturdy taproots often sustain them for decades as lowly shrubs. Most of them eventually die unless they begin to receive some sunlight. But if by chance such a shrubby oak becomes blessed with a sunny opening to the sky—as when an overshadowing neighbor dies—it draws from the reserve energy in its taproot and rapidly shoots up into a sapling, then into a slim pole with a narrow crown.

At this stage the oak—or almost any forest tree with sunlight overhead—will rid itself of lower branches whose leaves are not exposed to the sunlight. This process, natural pruning, makes for clear wood whose annual rings will grow over earlier knotholes; it is necessary for growth of a high-quality commercial tree. The same individual, if it were growing in a field, would receive sunlight from all directions and retain

In this timber, the aging process has begun to cause a decrease in production of board-feet

most of its lower limbs; it would develop a graceful spread but no commercial value.

After a forest tree reaches full height and is able to open the wide umbrella of a leafy crown, it is now ready to put maximum energy into production of board-feet. It attains its fastest growth in diameter. But eventually, as inherent vigor begins to lessen with aging, this last increment of growth diminishes; annual growth rings become narrower. In white oak this occurs at about 150 years; in most other trees it is sooner. It means, in any case, that although the tree still dominates a piece of the forest; it no longer produces many board-feet.

A mature tree is a reservoir of energy as well as a storehouse of wood. When that energy begins to be expended in fighting the decay of aging, it can no longer be directed toward growth. To an observant forester, the tree now becomes overaged. This means that if the forest in which it grows is primarily commercial, the tree needs to be harvested.

The growth pattern just described is typical of a mature forest. Where considerable logging has already occurred, however, or the land was previously cleared for farming, the situation proves entirely different.

After intensive logging, such as clearcutting, the forest will renew itself like a weed patch. Release of soil moisture and minerals from the demands of mature trees, plus plenty of sunlight, will encourage a jungle of seedling trees, shrubs, and herbs. All will begin growth with equal status. But the trees will quickly overtop and suppress lesser plants and begin to crowd each other. It will then be only a matter of time before there are too many trees, each one suffering competition from others the same age; some will die, but the growth rate of others will be retarded. Intensive logging, though it encourages rapid growth of new trees, sooner or later requires that they be thinned out to insure maximum growth in board-feet. Clearcutting demands intensive forest management.

Deciduous-forest renewal tends to be much slower on abandoned farmland than where logging has just occurred. Soil structure degenerates after years of cultivation, so the new forest must rebuild its foundation. This means, essentially, a slow accumulation of soil organic matter by a series of changes in plant types. The process is aptly called plant succession.

Bare land once occupied by deciduous forest will first go through a weedy stage, and then a brushy stage, before trees will successfully return. Early successional trees are seldom of the same species as later ones. In soils of limestone origin the first woody invader may be redcedar, not even a deciduous tree. Cleared valleys may be invaded by groves of cottonwood or silver maple. Various hill soils may encourage sweetgum, ashes, sassafras, certain hickories, or even elm. In any case, if the land continues undisturbed by man, successional trees will be replaced by more permanent, dominant species such as beech, sugar maple, and oaks. Yet the entire cycle is incredibly slow; from abandoned farmland to stable, mature forest may take more than two centuries. There is a worthy lesson in all this. It is patience and restraint. The man who strips forestland merely because of a jump in log prices, or to make pasture for currently high-priced cattle, may be making a mistake. He may temporarily fatten his bank account and shortchange his future, or that of his heirs.

A deciduous forest needs to sustain a healthy balance between growth and death processes, between the demands of commerce and those of other values. Man's manipulations of nature must never be hurried, or based on short-term goals; trees grow too slowly. Perhaps the first principle of good forest management is to understand just how a forest grows. □

THE AWAKENING

F or nearly six months of winter, the green life of the
deciduous forest has been in retreat. So have many of
the animals that depend upon it; they have either mi-
grated south or have remained in hibernation. Since last year's
foliage was discarded, trees and shrubs have secured their
hopes for spring in billions of tightly wrapped buds and in the
sap within their roots. Spring now needs to reawaken the
green life, start it anew, but the alarm clock it triggers is
sometimes premature.

Animals of the forest, and human visitors as well, are often
fooled by balmy days and southerly breezes of late winter.
Though terribly eager for spring, they are sent hurrying back
to shelter. Hibernators such as the groundhog go back to their

dens while we delay our outdoor plans and recheck our supply of heating fuel. But most plants cannot afford the luxury of premature awakenings, for once they actually start growing, they have no way to retreat from any threat of freezing. They may indeed freeze back on rare occasions, yet what they have learned through eons of evolutionary adaptations is to disregard fickle weather and instead respond to an alarm clock of celestial events.

Nothing in the forest experience is as eternally dependable as seasonal changes in day-length. As the earth orbits around the sun and its tilt begins to favor the northern hemisphere, days grow longer and nights shorter. Then the plants activate certain hormones in response to lengthening days and growth processes get their timely start. And although all plants produce such hormones, each species is adapted to its own particular schedule. This means that arrival of the vernal equinox, on March 21, has no special meaning to a plant unless its particular alarm clock is set precisely for the date when daytime equals nighttime. There is not, in other words, a certain magical day when the forest awakens to spring; each form of life has its own timetable.

Among the first forms awakened are certain mosses that exhibit tiny, inconspicuous sporing structures just an inch or so above the forest floor. Next comes an entire pageant of wildflowers which blossom, absorb sunlight, and complete most of their green growth before leaves develop in the forest canopy to blot out the sun. They include such favorites as Dutchman's breeches, bloodroot, toothwort, adder's tongue, and several species of violets. All of these blossom early, which tends to make them more resistant to freezing than longer-day plants. Depending upon local weather and latitude, they can be seen in deciduous woodlands from mid-March until mid-April. Though a late spell of cold weather can sometimes delay their emergence, an unusually early spell of warm weather will not bring them out before their proper day-length. And with regard to latitude, it is generally considered that spring advances northward at roughly 100 miles for every 10 days.

Migrating songbirds of the forest are also attuned, in their own ways, to lengthening days. Their reproductive organs enlarge in spring, releasing hormones that trigger their urge to fly northward from wherever they spent the winter. The exact secrets of bird navigation may still be in doubt, but they do return to nesting grounds on predictable time schedules. Yet nature is never perfect; if they are greeted by frigid weather

American or common toad emerging from hibernation

Yellow lady's-slipper; this rare orchid blooms when the leaves are emerging on forest trees

Redbud tree in bloom; note seedpods from previous year

Some of spring's earliest mosses exhibiting their tiny sporing structures

at their destinations, their instincts will not send them back, and so they occasionally suffer near-starvation in late snowstorms.

Hibernating animals, because they can easily retreat in cold weather, tend not to depend upon increasing day length. They are attuned to the whims of weather. The groundhog is aroused by warming sun and a gnawing hunger for new, succulent greenery. Tiny spring peepers and chorus frogs sing loudly and early where sunlight has warmed the water in shallow pools, but are aroused later from deep pools where water temperature is slower to rise; they also plunge back into the mud bottom with each temporary return of winter. Insects that hibernate as adults, such as honeybees and the lovely mourning cloak butterfly, become active on warm, sunny days but return to dormancy in frigid weather.

Slowly, each to its own schedule, trees begin to absorb soil moisture through new root hairs and to send it upward. Here again, length of day determines the timing for each species' rising fountain of sap.

Willows, elms, and silver maples in the valleys betray their awakening at about the same time as early wildflowers and some three weeks before oaks, hickories, and other trees of the ridges and slopes. They do so by exhibiting countless tiny flowers that consist of threadlike stamens and pinhead-size pistils but not petals. They are pollinated by wind and so have no need for either showy petals or nectar to attract insects; this is just as well, for there are not many pollinating insects so early in the spring. But the same trees may attract other, much larger creatures to their flowers. Squirrels, now hungering for a change after winter's diet of nuts and acorns, often teeter on the ends of branches just to nibble on flowers and swelling buds.

By this time there are many forest creatures busy with reproduction. Cottontail rabbits, in grass-lined cups within the forest floor, are already caring for first litters; white-footed mice may be doing the same, in or under rotting, fallen trees. Female foxes are giving birth to their pups. Groundhogs have only recently mated.

Many events of the forest spring, even if not timed to lengthening days, are synchronized in some way with each other, and for obvious reasons. Leaf-eating insects do not emerge until there is foliage for them to eat; songbirds of the trees do not normally arrive from the south in advance of foliage and insects.

The earliest songbird migrants are invariably ground-feeders

A mayapple's leaves use new spring warmth to soar above the plant's blossom

which scratch for seeds or insects in the forest carpet of dead leaves. Towhees fill brushy places with cheerful notes. White-throated sparrows, passing northward, grace our woodlands with plaintive whistles as we admire early wildflowers. Hermit thrushes, also transient, pass nearly unnoticed because they seldom sing their flute-like song before arriving at far northern nesting grounds. Resident robins, however, have sung for weeks, and they begin to shape their mud-lined nests as sap moves up to swell the buds on all the trees.

The sap now surges up like a fountain within wood cells—both new cells and those up to several years old—just inside the cambium, which produces both wood and inner bark. It pushes into buds and expands their countless embryonic cells, inflating them like microscopic balloons. The year's leaf crop is about to develop.

No single plant heralds the final, glorious surge of spring better than the flowering dogwood. This small, shade-tolerant tree, so typical of our deciduous forests, expands four gray bracts surrounding its modest flowers until they seem to be broad white petals. The actual tiny flowers, including yellow petals, are thus boldly advertised for pollination by insects. Other small trees exhibit early, showy blossoms in deciduous woods; they include serviceberry, redbud, wild plum, and the silver bell tree of southern states.

One week after its bracts are fully open, the white of dogwood becomes obscured by emergence of new leaves on nearly all forest trees. The buds of some, notably the shagbark hickory, swell to the size of a robin's egg before fully opening; other buds such as those of elms, maples, and the black cherry, all show delicate new leaves from the moment of opening. Even at this season, oaks offer a hint of the brilliant colors they will exhibit in autumn. The new downy leaves of white and red oak blush with reddish pigments before sunlight stimulates the development of their green chlorophyll.

Many forest trees, just at the time of leaf emergence, also produce their flowers. Some people are surprised to learn that such trees as oaks and hickories bloom in the spring—or at all, for that matter. Yet a tree cannot develop seeds without flowers any more than a tomato plant can bear fruit without first blossoming. The wind-pollinated flowers of many trees are obscure simply because they develop at the same time as leaves and because they have no showy petals.

All of the oaks produce greenish, staminate tassels from which the wind extracts billions of microscopic pollen cells; the pistillate flowers which will develop into acorns are mean-

*Bloodroot—an early spring
wildflower*

*One of many small, toadstool-type
mushrooms growing on fallen
limbs and other forest debris
in spring*

Ohio buckeye in full bloom

*Leaves and staminate tassels of the
red oak*

*Pastel-tinted oak leaves unfurling at
the height of spring*

Leaves of white oak, just emerging

while hardly bigger than pinheads. The same applies to hickories. The flowers of cottonwood and white ash are more conspicuous, but the male and female parts are on separate trees. As the foliage of a forest grows into a dense canopy, wind-pollinated flowers are no longer very effective; the free blowing-about of dustlike cells is then hindered by all the leaves. Later-blossoming trees—the catalpa, the buckeye, the locusts, and the magnificent tulip poplar—all exhibit showy petals and are pollinated by insects.

Meanwhile, just above the forest floor is a continuing pageant of wildflowers, each species enjoying the sunlight which is even now being blotted out by developing foliage high above. The earliest have faded and are now replaced by mayapples, blue phlox, wild iris, bluebells, late-blooming violets, and finally the rare and showy lady's-slipper orchids. A variety of ferns also uncurl their lacy fiddleheads.

Now the rapidly leafing, flowering plant life brings out a new crop of insects. Chewing caterpillars hatch from masses of autumn-deposited eggs or emerge from hibernation to attack all types of foliage; they attract their share of predatory insects and spiders. Live-born aphids in untold billions cluster to suck the fresh plant juices; they attract ants which tend and milk them of mysterious secretions. And all, in turn, serve to refuel waves of hungry songbirds just arriving from the south.

As many as two dozen species of tiny, colorful warblers may brighten the canopy of a deciduous forest at the height of spring, some arriving to nest and others—such as the blackburnian, black-throated green, and magnolia warblers—just passing through to evergreen forests in the far North. The undergrowth, meanwhile, entertains its own resident species: the Kentucky and worm-eating warblers and the ovenbird; also wrens and several kinds of sparrows. And in addition, either staying to nest or migrating through, are numerous species of flycatchers, thrushes, vireos, orioles, and tanagers. Each one enriches the forest morning and evening with characteristic song, and all help in controlling the new prolific crop of insects.

Perhaps one year out of 10, just at the height of spring, weather falls back into a fickle mood and brings a quick touch of winter. Cool, gray days are followed by a clear and frigid morning that fills low-lying areas with frost. Trees and shrubs find that their inherent confidence in celestial events has been betrayed; their new tender foliage is killed back and blackens. Though not a typical occurrence, this demands a completely new start of the growth processes. Mature trees and shrubs suffer little from such late frosts, for they usually have ample food stored in roots and trunk; but it does tend to kill quite a few seedling plants. The struggle for survival in a forest applies to all types of life, and in many ways.

Each year, however, there comes that time when the last danger of frost is gone. Spring is then over; summer has arrived.

The most dramatic, action-filled time of spring is always when trees are rapidly filling their crowns with new sets of pastel-tinted leaves. It is also the loveliest. But the most memorable day is the one when we discover that very first sign of a forest's awakening. It marks the beginning of life's annual tide of growing and multiplying, a cycle as dependable as the earth's eternal orbit around the sun. ☐

LIFE AMONG THE LIMBS

Most of the living substance in a forest—in all the varied forms that it takes—originates from the green crowns of trees. This is where countless chlorophyll-bearing leaves, each one a tiny, living factory, produce food by photosynthesis. Some of this food is converted into wood and other plant tissues, some is kept in reserve as starch or in its primary sugary form in the sap, and the remainder is used to fuel the living processes of the tree.

Only a small percent of the living substance in a forest can originate below crown height. This is because of limited light penetration within shadowy realms beneath. It is no exaggeration that the limbs of a forest support its most basic life-sustaining process. It all happens wherever photosynthesis occurs.

45

Each leaf draws water and mineral elements from the soil by way of roots, trunk, and limbs. It absorbs carbon dioxide from the atmosphere through thousands of stomates, or pores, on its underside. Beneath transparent cells on its upper surface are several more layers of cells, all containing the enzyme chlorophyll. This remarkable substance traps energy from most light rays—except the green rays, which it reflects—received from the sun, some 92 million miles away. It then serves to lock the energy into bonds, or atomic attachments, which assemble glucose molecules. Finally the process releases oxygen through the stomata, though some is retained to fuel the metabolism of the tree.

The raw materials, energy source, and end-products of photosynthesis have all been identified. Their various components have been accurately measured. But what really happens in the food-manufacturing process—the intricate details of numerous chemical steps—is so complex that no team of scientists, aided by the best of laboratory facilities, has yet been able to duplicate the entire sequence outside of a living leaf. There is no humanly devised substitute for photosynthesis.

We know that in order for the process to work, essential minerals must be lifted to the limbs of trees with a flow of water. We realize that depleted soils cannot assure this. We know also that air that enters the stomata must not be polluted. Beyond these facts, all we can do is appreciate the canopy of the forest as the source of its living substance. And we can see that it is where animal life seeks its first source of nourishment.

The first in line are generally insects. In spring, from the moment countless buds unfurl into leaves, chewing and sucking insects begin to feed. Among the most visible are caterpillars, the larvae of butterflies and moths. They grow in all colors and shapes, some smooth as satin and others armed with turrets of threatening bristles. Each species requires its own type of leaf and proper season for growth. If caterpillars are collected and caged for observation, they will starve unless given the right kind of leaf. Yet no species of forest tree ever fully escapes the ravages of caterpillars. The perfect leaves of spring are mostly chewed into tatters by autumn.

Other well-known chewers include the spindly, camouflaged walking stick and the leafy-winged katydids that fill summer nights with their monotonous sawing and buzzing sounds. Various types of beetles also attack the foliage of trees. Then there are the gall insects, most of them tiny flies or wasps, which do strange things to plant tissues. They secrete hormone-like substances that cause diagnostic growths on leaves or twigs.

Aphids on the underside of a tulip-poplar leaf are nourished by the sugary food manufactured for the tree. They use needlelike tubes for the extraction

The tiny creatures find refuge inside these growths while feeding on the cancerlike tissues they have generated.

Much less noticeable than tattered leaves or grotesque galls are the punctures left by sucking insects, particularly aphids. They are sap thieves. Each one has a needlelike tube with which to draw upon the sugary products of photosynthesis. Reproduction in aphids is such that, from May through August, females make up the entire population of most species. These give birth to live young, and what they lack in size they make up in numbers. Finally, in late summer, winged adults of both sexes make their appearance and mate. Only then do the females produce eggs in typical insect fashion.

Were it not for natural enemies, the reproductive powers of forest insects would enable them to destroy the very trees they depend upon. Occasionally, in localized areas, some types become quite damaging. Yet this situation invariably leads to rapid population growth of their enemies. The great diversity of life in a deciduous forest nearly guarantees this natural control.

Thus, we might say, second in line to receive nourishment among the limbs are those predators and parasites that feed on vegetarian insects. In control of aphids, these include green and golden lacewings and ladybird beetles. Moths and other flying types are trapped in the webs of spiders. In addition, many potential leaf-destroyers yield their substance, little by little, to parasites that deposit eggs upon their immature forms; most abundant of these are the various species of braconid wasps.

By far the best-known of all predators upon insects are songbirds. So long as they can avoid caterpillars with poisonous bristles or a disagreeable taste, birds are seldom choosy in their diets. They leave the unpalatable types to other agents of control.

In observing the insectivorous birds of the forest, it is interesting to note how each species has its own niche, or means of livelihood. Like a well-coordinated police force, each type has its own particular beat. Colorful warblers and the vireos glean small insects from the outer foliage; some work high in the crowns of dominant trees while others search the shadowy realm of understory vegetation. Nuthatches probe the bark of limbs and trunk to find eggs and pupae. Flycatchers wait on dead branches below the canopy to lunge for flying insects and snatch them on the wing. At night the whippoorwill weaves among the trees to scoop flying moths and beetles into its wide, bristle-rimmed gape.

The substance and the energy of these birds are derived from the trees. Their distinctive songs are fueled indirectly via the sun, through the photosynthetic process, and directly by the

The lacewing, seldom noticed except at night when attracted to lights, is an important predator of sap-sucking aphids

Caterpillars get nourishment directly from leaves. This one, on a tulip poplar, will develop into a tiger swallowtail butterfly

The katydid, with its familiar summer night song, can be recognized as a male by the brown singing organ atop thorax

A robin acts as a predator in the woodland food chain in order to bring insects to the nest for feeding to newly hatched young

insects that have nourished themselves from the greenery.

The leaves are not the only source of food that trees provide for creatures of the forest. Whatever the leaves produce that is converted into wood and bark is also potential nourishment, either directly or indirectly. The beaver that fells a tree by a stream, the woodpecker that excavates dead wood for beetle grubs, the lowly termites that finally reduce a fallen giant to organic rubble—each gets its share from the same original source.

The wood created high above ground is just as eagerly sought as that which eventually crashes down, even if it is not as vulnerable or accessible.

As each twig on a tree lengthens, and new wood is added over that of the previous year, a protective sheath of bark also develops. This thickens as the limb grows in diameter. It serves as armor that resists bacteria, fungi, and wood-boring insects.

Whenever a dead limb breaks from a tree, as by natural pruning, it leaves a circular scar—a potential knothole— through the bark. The next year's annual ring of new wood is then stimulated to overgrow the scar. If the scar is of small diameter, healing can occur before damaging organisms have a chance to invade the wood. But large trees have a disadvantage in this respect. Young ones drop small limbs that leave tiny scars, but mature trees are apt to drop much bigger limbs, causing scars too wide for successful healing. In this way older trees fall behind in a lengthy battle against invading bacteria, fungi, and boring insects.

Regardless of age or size, a tree begins to lose inherent vigor whenever it accumulates scars it can no longer heal with new growth. This may occur at age 30 in the case of a wind-damaged willow, or not for a century with a sturdy oak. Invasion of the inner, dead heartwood, first by bacteria and next by fungi, slowly softens it and allows easy access for wood-borers. And though the tree can for a time effectively protect its outer, living shell from inner infections, heart rot gradually weakens the supporting structure.

So in the process stretching from glucose originally produced by leaves, to cellulose and other ingredients of woody tissue, food and energy are eventually transferred to decomposers. Slow as this process might be, it ultimately brings the tree crashing down.

Though hardly visible to us, the inner rot of a standing tree never fails to attract secondary consumers. Woodpeckers are the best examples. They seldom do harm to solid wood, for they have nothing to extract from it. But their soundings with chisellike beaks have an uncanny way of locating wood-boring

Fruits and seeds of forest trees, such as these developing acorns of a white oak, are made possible by the synthesizing processes

Many insects are picky in their eating habits. Larvae of hackberry butterfly feed only on leaves of hackberry tree

Among lesser-known fruits of the deciduous forest is the pawpaw. It is edible when ripe and is comparable to a banana in taste

A pileated woodpecker uses diseased portion of a white ash for nesting. Note fungus growth at left, level with cavity

insects, even under healthy-looking bark. By drilling holes in the diseased portions of trees, woodpeckers may open new avenues for invading organisms. They also excavate nesting cavities, commonly in exposed knotholes left by fallen limbs and on diseased portions of otherwise healthy trees.

Some woodpeckers, particularly the crow-size pileated, may use the same cavity for several nesting seasons. Most species, however, prefer to chisel new ones every year. Thus they are worthy home-builders for other wildlife. Crested flycatchers, nuthatches, chickadees, and titmice seek abandoned woodpecker holes. So do various species of squirrels, which often do some gnawing to enlarge the cavities.

Most of the above-named tenants unwittingly pay a small rent for the privilege. The songbirds share with other predators in the important task of controlling summer's multiplying insects. As mentioned in Chapter 1, squirrels bury nuts and acorns in large numbers and do not always find them later; some of these buried treasures grow into trees. The ones the squirrels do consume, like the seeds and fruits of all forest trees, represent another category of food that originates from the limbs above.

Entrances into tree trunks and limbs occasionally heal over with new wood from outside. Usually, however, animal tenants work successfully to prevent this. The chisel-toothed squirrels are particularly adept at gnawing to enlarge cavities. And because the heartwood inside is already dead, it is impossible for damage there to be reduced in any way. Thus we find that larger tenants, such as barred owls and raccoons, take over dens that have become too roomy for birds and squirrels.

The den trees of a forest may not contribute to the financial income of an owner seeking to sell wood products. But a generous scattering of such trees, even if too old and damaged for harvest, will almost guarantee the presence of interesting wildlife forms—one factor that makes any woodland attractive to outdoor enthusiasts.

The diversity of a typical deciduous forest is one of its greatest assets. The many species of trees provide a varied menu for the animals that inhabit them. Yet it should be with awe, and perhaps a bit of reverence, that we look up to the green canopy that crowns the forest all summer. It is there that the sun's energy and the raw materials of photosynthesis are miraculously assembled into the substance of life. □

THE LIVING FLOOR

Years ago a youth-camp counselor led some boys, including me, on what he called an upside-down hike. He took us to the woods and soon had us turning over rocks and fallen logs to discover what lived underneath. I was fascinated and have been snooping around the world of woodland recyclers ever since.

Creatures of the woodland floor are bankers for the green world above. When broadleaved trees drop their autumn crops of gold, or when death brings the old trees crashing down, countless decomposers are waiting to process the remains. Included are bacteria, fungi, earthworms, beetles, and termites; predators such as centipedes, spiders, and shrews feed on the decomposers. Final remains, as fertilizer, are doled out as dividends for the future of the woodland.

The economy of a woodland, as of any natural community, is based entirely on recycling. There is, of course, a loss of energy common to the living of all life. Yet this poses no problem; the green canopy of summer woods can capture all the solar energy it needs through chlorophyll-tinted leaves.

Where trees have all been removed from the land, the soil's nutrient dividends are washed away by heavy rains. They cannot be reinvested in the same woodland. In such cases, also, no more solar energy can be captured until a new crop of greenery once more raises leafy arms to the sun.

In a healthy woodland the nutrients and energy are distributed through food chains, as from acorn to mouse to hawk. Yet the eventual return of their dividends to the soil has been likened to food chains in reverse. Portions of the acorn not usable by the mouse are reduced by molds and bacteria; parts of the mouse not usable by the hawk will help a fern grow or a wildflower to blossom.

Woodland recycling takes time, but nature has infinite patience. Dead leaves decompose faster than fallen logs, bringing this thought to mind: what if autumn crops of gold did not decompose at all? Obviously they would pile up from year to year until they would bury entire woodlands. They would be like our own industrial trash, a monumental accumulation of waste that provides no dividends for the future.

In the woods near my home, nature requires three years to reduce autumn's fallen leaves to humus, or woodland fertilizer. Decomposition starts the spring following leaf-fall and involves the work of leaf-mining insects, snails, slugs, wood lice, millipedes, and roaches. Fungi do their share of the work when moisture is plentiful; their pallid threads weave in and out unseen until finally, as though to prove their special identities, they erupt into the spore producers we know as mushrooms or toadstools. The end product of dead leaves, humus, is then passed through bodies of earthworms to be cast upward in a perpetual plowing operation.

If leaf decomposition seems slow, that of fallen logs may seem endless. A hickory log may rot in five years; a large fallen oak may require two decades. Fungi, termites, and beetles do much of the work; but most fascinating to me are the slime molds.

I had read about slime molds long before actually seeing them. To observe them in their natural state demands literally crawling in rain-soaked woods. They are jelly-like blobs that flow at the rate of a half-inch per hour and engulf bacteria like

This rotting log, a fallen tree, is a typical scene of the woodland floor, shown here in spring and autumn

a wet sponge picking up crumbs. Enlarged upon by imagination, they are fitting subjects for science fiction; it is probably fortunate that slime molds are measured only in inches. But when the weather dries out, their slithering is over. Then they stream into the open and, even while shriveling away, produce hundreds of sporing structures the size of pinheads. After releasing a legacy in reproductive spores, slime molds disappear until another spell of rain once more unleashes their slimy wanderings.

Most important in recycling fallen trees are the termites. Notorious for eating finished lumber as well as dead trees, they seem addicted to the principle of robbing man to repay nature. Yet their success depends entirely upon henchmen within their gut. Termites cannot digest cellulose, the major component of wood, and so they harbor microscopic protozoans in their stomachs to do the chemical digesting and to share in the meal. This strange partnership is assured for all members of the colony by a ritual of trading regurgitated, protozoan-laden morsels of food, and occurs from the time of hatching.

In the termite caste system workers and soldiers, plodding blindly through tunnels of their own making, live only to serve their queen, a perpetual egg machine. Yet the American subterranean termite, our most common species, can actually manage without a queen. A friend of mine in the termite control business has kept a colony of this species isolated in a gallon jar for 17 years. The jar has a tight metal lid with a small hole in the center; a block of wood over the hole, replaced occasionally with some moisture, is all the colony needs to survive. My friend has never seen a queen in the jar and doubts that one was originally inserted with the colony. What keeps them going, he feels certain, is that subterranean termites can delegate egg-laying to a sexually mature member known as a secondary reproductive. It makes me wonder if a termite colony, like a trust fund that operates on dividends, could maintain itself in perpetuity.

However long its perpetuation, a termite colony can surely boast an ancient lineage. It is believed that the tiny decomposers of wood have thrived in essentially the same form for at least 250 million years; the henchmen in their stomachs must be just as ancient. Other primitive creatures of the woodland floor include the silverfish which live in rotting logs and neglected books, wood lice which roll into tiny pills, and the many-legged millipedes and centipedes.

Millipedes are proof that an animal's speed has no relationship to number of legs. In spite of four legs per body segment,

Pinhead-size sporing structures of a typical slime mold dot the surface of a rotting log

A Gastropod, which means "belly-footed", the snail has a broad, tapered foot on which it glides

The saprophytic pinesap has no chlorophyll and cannot manufacture its food as do green plants

Pallid threads of fungi attack leaves that fell from trees the previous autumn. Photo was taken in May

Like most roaches, this one might leave its hiding place at night for short woodland flights

The reddish band of tissue around this earthworm is the clitellum, which later will slip off over the head to become an egg case

The underside of a fallen log reveals a garden of several fungus species and a small millipede that was probably feeding there

Workers of the American subterranean termite, the most common species in the U.S. outside the Deep South. Termites have thrived in essentially the same form for at least 250 million years

The camel cricket, also called cave cricket, is common under rotting logs

A least shrew, about the size of an acorn, reacts "like a mad tiger" when sense of touch tells him food is near

or a total of over 300, they are recognized by their laboriously slow movement. Their success and great numbers within the woodland floor are due to simple scavenging diets and an ability to secrete offensive odors. One common species, however, offers a pleasant surprise when disturbed; it smells deliciously like fresh almonds.

Whereas millipedes are harmless scavengers, centipedes are quick and fearless predators. Their one pair of legs per segment are long and agile and their two stinging claws are, in some species, quite poisonous. The way they squeeze their flat bodies into tight places in search of prey gives me remote pangs of claustrophobia; yet I know they are perfectly suited for hunting worms and insects in the dark world below our feet.

There is one animal of the woodland floor that outdoes the centipede in predatory energy. It is the shrew. Recently I kept a fully grown least shrew, no bigger than a white oak acorn, in a small terrarium. It was almost constantly moving, ever searching for a potential meal. Even during rare moments of rest, it would raise and vibrate its tiny snout every few seconds. What good this did I am not sure, for shrews are not only blind, they have a weak sense of smell. But what my shrew lacked in certain senses, it overcame in touch; when I dropped an earthworm on its snout it reacted like a mad tiger. It killed and ate ravenously. Once it devoured three worms twice its length in a half-hour. Shrews spend most of their frantic lives seeking food and, in the process, may consume several times their body weight each day in worms, beetles, snails, slugs, and occasionally even other shrews. Though they may number several dozen per acre of woodland, their eating habits pose no threat to the millions of dwellers in their mysterious world.

Trying to count the dwellers in an acre of woodland floor would be like trying to count individual leaves in a forest, or atoms within a leaf—impossible in any case. The recyclers are a complete community in themselves. Each type is a specialist in processing some particular dead animal, or leaf, or fallen log. Whether by divine purpose or by trial and error of countless centuries, nature guarantees that the remains of the dead will provide fertile dividends for the future. In the urgent need to solve our own problems of recycling, we would do well to learn from the example of the woodland recyclers. ☐

The centipede is a quick and fearless predator. Note the poisonous stinging claws on either side of its head

THE WOODLAND STREAM

An ample supply of moisture, well-distributed throughout the year, is the lifeblood of any forest. Delivered as
rain or snow, it sustains the trees, lesser plants, and all
varieties of animal life. It also joins springs and rivulets into
streams, then finally into rivers. In this process the forest serves
as a watershed.

By definition, watersheds are any areas drained by streams
and rivers. Small watersheds combine into larger ones. But the
way they function is really a compromise between how much
water they hold back and how much they release. Low runoff
may at times make water less available for downstream uses
but, in the long run, will provide better seasonal distribution.
Too much runoff causes soil erosion and downstream flooding

and makes the land above unable to hold back water for droughty times. Generally, the slower the water moves through a watershed, the better; in addition to protecting the land, slow movement enhances the many values of woodland streams.

To understand the origins of any stream, an observer needs to follow it from small beginnings. This means starting with the basics of precipitation—raindrops and snowflakes.

Summer raindrops falling on a deciduous forest lose much of their momentum by spattering and bouncing off foliage, from the treetops down to shrubs and even low-growing herbs. As much as one-fourth of this moisture may then evaporate directly from leaf and branch surfaces. In an undisturbed forest, rain reaching the ground is cushioned by a carpet of forest litter and humus; how much of it soaks in depends on the amount of spongy humus, the structure of the soil beneath, and how hard it rains. Absorption is faster in soils with coarse particles, such as sand and gravel, than in tightly compacted types of smaller particles, such as clay. But even the most porous soil can become temporarily saturated after heavy rains; then, of course, runoff is greatly increased.

As much as half of summer's rainfall—excluding runoff from extraordinarily heavy downpours—is drawn up by roots of trees and released to the air by transpiration from stomata, or leaf pores. This is a factor contributing to the high relative humidity typical of all green, growing forests. The trees, in effect, help to maintain their own requirements for a humid environment.

Loss of moisture to the air by winter-dormant trees is almost negligible, but the ground runoff of rain is usually much greater. The condition with snow is different: some of it tends to evaporate directly, but because it tends to melt more slowly under partial shade of bare trees than it does in an open field, a larger percentage of it is likely to soak deeply into the soil.

Within the span of any year, a healthy forest serves to hold back much of the precipitation received by its watershed. But where the land has been scarred by human activity—by repeated burning, overgrazing by livestock, cultivation of slopes in clearings, or by sloppy logging practices—the runoff is accelerated, valuable topsoil is lost, and normal flooding is grossly increased. This is the sad, hidden price we pay too often for careless stewardship of the land.

The flow of a typical woodland stream comes partly from direct runoff, but it also comes from soil seepage at the base of slopes and from deeper sources. Falling rain has a way of ab-

Early spring comes to a stream of the kind popular with canoeists and campers

sorbing carbon dioxide from the air and forming a very weak solution of carbonic acid. Over centuries of time, as water seeps into cracks of rock strata—particularly limestone—this acid slowly dissolves rock surfaces to enlarge channels of flow; such are the sources of caves, springs, and underground rivers that eventually surface.

The more devious its pathways through rock and soil, the slower and more constant is the water supply feeding a woodland stream. Some of the water does not even surface; it replenishes the deeper watertable, which sustains wells for human use, often far from the original watershed.

Unless a beginning woodland stream originates from a sizable spring, it will seldom maintain a continuous flow. A young stream's arteries tend to be seasonal. But anyone seeking to study the life of an infant stream should not ignore its temporary waters. Such places illustrate the principle that the lowest forms of life are often the best adapted for surviving extreme conditions. In nature, to be small and simple can be an advantage.

Though fish and frogs may shun the temporary stream, tiny creatures can survive as eggs in the gravel of dried pool beds, as can spores of algae upon which the creatures will feed when water returns. Spring rains will rejuvenate the small life gone dormant in dry streams of autumn. Gravelly pools will then become lined with algae and grow crowded with tiny crustaceans and insects; minnows may then even migrate upstream to feed upon them. There is some life in every woodland pool, however temporary.

A person lost in an upland forest is wise to follow the first ravine or drainage downward. In a deciduous forest such a course invariably leads to permanent water within a couple of miles; here the wanderer can chance a drink. Assuming the watershed above is undisturbed and uninhabited by humans, the stream is likely to be quite drinkable. What makes any natural source of water polluted and unsafe, in other words, is activity by humans and domestic livestock in the watershed.

A permanent, unpolluted woodland stream is one of the most attractive havens in all of nature. It should be protected as a worthy part of every sizable forest area. The unique plant life along its banks—whether sycamore, birch, willow, and cottonwood trees, or simply alder bushes—should be left alone to guard against cutting erosion; too often this is not done.

Such a stream, spawned by the forest watershed, harbors a wealth of aquatic life. Its water, rich in nutrients from the forest soil and from accumulated organic matter, provides first for

The crayfish scavenges in the shallow water of many streams

Cloudless sulphur butterfly drinks in moisture from a muddy spot on the shore of a woodland stream

Spring peeper fills early spring nights with its plaintive music

Immature green heron waits by the side of a stream for darting movements of an unwary minnow or tadpole

In its immature stages, the damselfly spends its whole time in the water

plant life. The small amount of greenery in swift-flowing riffles is mostly restricted to algae growing on boulders and gravel. But even small plant life supports a variety of specialized insects—some that eat the algae directly and others that prey upon each other. These insects include the streamlined, rock-hugging nymphs of mayflies, stoneflies, dobsonflies, and also caddisfly larvae, which surround themselves with sticks or pebbles held together with silk.

In pools between riffles, where water flow is gentler, there are usually beds of rooted water plants. These plants serve as food for snails, tadpoles, and minnows. Water striders and whirligig beetles skim the water surface for tiny insects that fall from trees; down below, predatory dragonfly nymphs await their turn. Crayfish scavenge along the bottom while mussels burrow through its silty deposits. Trout or bass—depending on water temperature—lurk in the pools and at the lower end of riffles; their food may include anything mentioned above.

Anyone curious enough to explore with net and sifting pan, or with a small seine, will be amazed at the stream's diversity of life forms. Differences between creatures found in pools and those found in riffles can be especially revealing.

The stream's life is an integral part of the forest. Food chains link the aquatic environment with the world above its surface:

A mated wood-duck hen feeds on water plants, then produces eggs and incubates them in a hollow tree not far from the bank;

a moth, its caterpillar earlier nourished by oak leaves, falls into a pool and is eaten by a dragonfly nymph;

a raccoon that sleeps by day in a hollow tree dabbles in the water by night in search of crayfish;

A green heron competes with bass for tadpoles, which it feeds to a nestful of hungry nestlings in a nearby willow tree. Many life-threads from the stream are tied in some way to the trees.

The water in a typical woodland stream tends to remain quite cool, even during the heat of summer. Abundant shade from overhanging trees helps. But perhaps more important, especially where shallow water flows over riffles, is the constant cooling effect of a high rate of evaporation.

Yet only the coldest streams, either fed by sizable springs or originating in mountainous areas, can well support trout. This is because trout demand more oxygen than bass, and the colder the water, the more of this essential gas is held in solution. Even where riffles aerate the flow, trout can barely survive in water temperatures above 70° Fahrenheit. For this

Trees above a motionless pool provide the organic matter essential to the first stages of the food chain

reason they inhabit the coldest swift-flowing headwaters while bass tend to dominate the warmer stretches of water farther downstream. Both attract admiring fisherman wherever they thrive.

At whatever point a woodland stream has grown big enough to support trout or bass, or to float a canoe—this is where people begin to gather and to threaten it with abuses.

Camping areas and vacation developments are most popular where both fishing and boating are available. Headwaters are particularly attractive, because they tend to be cool and wild. Yet they do not always remain that way. On public lands, streamside developments are often restricted to widely spaced access roads and campsites; the same applies to lands owned by large, responsible lumber companies. There, problems are usually limited to the twin nuisances of litter and vandalism. But where the ownership is in small private holdings, threats of environmental abuse are greatly multiplied.

There is nothing so degrading to a stream's natural beauty— and to the purity of its water—than vacation cabin developments along the banks. These developments can spring up like unplanned subdivisions. Usually they are not served by adequate plumbing and their sewage finds its way into the stream. The decomposition of this sewage removes oxygen needed by the aquatic animals; unique life forms are destroyed, and normal food chains are broken. Where motorboats are used, oil slicks can add to the pollution.

And the cabin owners, though loving the natural surroundings, may rent to people who do not really care. These renters may dump their trash over the bank rather than haul it home. By this time the woodland stream has lost all its natural beauty; it is then just one more badly abused and degraded river.

Dams are another threat to woodland streams. The issues of small dams built on private lands—except for concern over structural safety—are of little moment to most people. But the large ones, federally funded and often located where they will inundate headwaters systems, are a different matter.

Arguments for building such dams often tend to place local economic promises and political pressures above all other considerations. One group begs flood protection for floodplain development; another tries to promote flatwater fun in a pristine setting. Voters in the project area are goaded with promises of economic growth and, in some cases, of needed energy to be produced by a hydroelectric generating plant below the dam. Stakes are always high for those local congressmen who support such projects.

*Tracks left in streamside soil by woodland creatures.
Above: wood duck. Below: raccoon*

*Rainbow trout, a favorite of fishermen, prefer cooler,
swifter upstream stretches*

*Tiger salamander, like all amphibians, breeds in
quiet pools of streams*

Those who oppose large dams have their arguments too, of course. They wish to preserve natural values, to enjoy canoeing and stream fishing, or simply to save taxpayers' dollars. Yet they seldom can generate the lobbying force of economic promoters. Strangely, in some recent cases, their strongest ally has proved to be the legal force of an Endangered Species Act intended to prevent the extinction of unusual life forms. Environmentalists have gone to court with evidence that certain species of plants or animals are endangered simply because the supporting stream communities are themselves threatened. The question is, how much should we sacrifice in things wild and natural for a dam?

Every headwater stream—because of soil, topography, climate, and the type of forest surrounding it—is unique. Each one might be considered worth preserving on its special merits. Perhaps we cannot justify saving every one—but too many such streams have already been destroyed by pollution and dams. □

Although the spring peeper breeds in water, the small toad lives in trees

ENEMIES

All forms of life have their enemies; they can threaten either the individual, the species, or the entire community. It makes a great deal of difference, however, whether an enemy is natural in origin or is the result of human activities. A deciduous forest can adapt to insect pests, ravaging fungi, and weather-related forces such as windstorms, floods, droughts, and occasional fires caused by lightning. But it can never adapt to destruction of soil foundations, poisoning by exotic chemicals, or to such human industry as paving the landscape with concrete.

In a healthy forest community, as mature trees die and are replaced by competing saplings, each species is able to adapt through survival of the fittest to all sorts of natural cycles and climatic changes. Slowly, century after century, an ever-changing balance of life keeps the forest going.

Consider the many species of insects that annually attack a community of trees. Each type has a certain time, place, and method of doing its work. Caterpillars, as they eat and grow larger, consume ever more foliage as the growing season progresses; aphids suck more sap from leaf-veins as they multiply through the summer; weevils eat out the seed parts of acorns shortly before they ripen; wood-boring beetles extend their tunnels in scarred, aging trees.

Yet all insect pests—except such aliens as the gypsy moth and Japanese beetle—seem to have their own enemies. For nearly every plant eater there is another insect that is either predatory or parasitic. And there are the insect-eating spiders, lizards, bats, and such birds as warblers in the treetops, woodpeckers on trunks and branches, sparrows at ground level where new seedlings must get their start, plus those birds that catch winged adults: flycatchers in daylight and whippoorwills at night. All of these predators, however, do not insure a constant balance; nature is never that perfect.

Trees are sometimes stripped of foliage by walking sticks, leaf-eating beetles, or caterpillars such as the fall webworm. Yet these infestations tend to occur mostly in late summer, when insect hordes mature in both size and number. By then the trees have usually completed their year's growth; they do not regenerate damaged parts; thus they expend less energy and save their reserves for the next year. Outbreaks of insect pests, if they recur in successive years, invariably generate counterattacks by their own enemies. Finally, those trees that may be killed by insects are the very young—too numerous for all to survive anyway—and those that are both aged and diseased.

Other living, natural enemies of forest trees are no worse than the insects. Many fungi can penetrate the scars of trees, especially the sizable scars of larger trees. Most are decomposers, which serve to gradually recycle nutrients locked into the dead heartwood of a forest. By the time a tree is old enough, or scarred enough, to suffer interior ravages by fungi, it is due for replacement by a younger, healthier one anyway.

As among insects, the only fungi that really threaten deciduous trees are the aliens. One example is the Dutch elm disease, carried by several species of bark beetles. Another is the chestnut blight, accidentally brought into the United States back at the turn of the century. Within a few decades it virtually eliminated what originally had been one of the

Lightning, when it does not kill a tree, will often cause a damaging scar from topmost limbs to the ground. This lightning damage occurred to a large shagbark hickory

finest, most useful of our native trees. Some chestnuts still endure, as sprouts which grow perhaps 10 feet high and may even produce seed, but these are blighted again and again; no longer do they ever grow into trees.

Weather is sometimes considered a serious enemy of the forest. Its long-term extension—that is, climate—is what changes the nature of a forest through the centuries. This is what happened after the last ice age, when retreating continental glaciers yielded to evergreen forests and then eventually to present-day deciduous types. But the slow processes of changing climate also adapt trees to the shorter cycles we know as seasonal weather. This works by survival of the fittest.

When drought comes to a deciduous forest, as it invariably does in recurring cycles, it acts as a sort of purge. Just as predators of the cottontail rabbit serve to cull out the surplus, the weak, and the diseased, drought does a comparable service for the forest.

One growing season of drought may kill large numbers of small, crowded trees that do not have the root systems to draw deep subsoil moisture; they will, of course, be replaced by some future crop of nuts, acorns, and other seeds. A second successive summer of drought will then likely eliminate the oldest, most diseased trees of the forest. But those that remain healthy—always descended from earlier generations that have adapted to drought—will merely suffer retarded growth until the wet years return.

What applies to purging effects of drought might also be true of other weather peculiarities. Ice storms occasionally blanket trees with layers of freezing rain. Those that are soft-wooded and those that are weakened, from whatever cause, then suffer the most damage.

Windstorms often damage or kill trees, especially if they are aged or exposed. Those growing in dense stands, where they tend to shield each other from sudden gusts, are less vulnerable than trees in open, windswept places. But where wind does not serve to thin out crowded stands, competition for sunlight, water and soil nutrients will eventually do the same. Here again, as in other ways, the forces within a healthy forest community tend to balance each other; if they are natural, they are not really enemies.

Fire is often viewed as a terrible enemy of the forest. Yet this is not always so. Deciduous trees, except during the most severe summer and autumn droughts, do not suffer burning of their crowns. Flames do not consume green foliage unless it is heavily wax-coated and highly flammable, as on many

Acorn weevils are tiny beetles that insert their eggs into ripening acorns; their larvae can destroy as much as 90% of an oak tree's seed potential

Cross section of white oak with "cat's-paw," or scar, resulting from a damaging ground fire; bacteria and fungi have invaded heartwood

Look closely at what's left of lower leaf, and you'll spot the walking stick, an insect that can multiply to huge populations which completely defoliate forest trees in the late summer

Cattle and deer can destroy a forest's undergrowth and reproductive potential. Browse line seen here was caused by overpopulation of whitetail deer

cone-bearing trees. A deciduous forest fire is usually limited to the ground. It does destroy leaf litter, fallen branches, dead trees, saplings, and undergrowth. If abundant fuel is available, it may also scorch the base of tree trunks and cause permanent fire-scars; trees beyond sapling size, however, usually survive such burns.

Eastern woodlands suffer the most damage when burned annually, as was long the custom in the southern Appalachian and Ozark hills regions. This woods burning was typically done in early spring, supposedly to destroy chiggers, snakes, and weed plants and to encourage grass to grow for cattle. But the reasoning was faulty. Woodlands never make good pasture for cattle; surface fires do not control animal pests and perennial weeds; the yearly loss of decomposing material and undergrowth does not help soil fertility, water-holding capacity, or wildlife cover. Fire—if used under carefully controlled conditions—can sometimes help seedling production in a forest where there is too much ground cover, but annual burning is never helpful.

A forest can, in the long run, cope with natural enemies including occasional lightning fires, but human activities are more likely to be harmful, sometimes even when they are not intended to be so.

In parks and refuges closed to hunting, where cougars and wolves have been exterminated as natural predators of deer, good human intentions often prove damaging. Deer tend to overpopulate such areas and eat every bit of foliage as high as they can reach; the evidence is clearly visible as a browse line throughout the forest. All undergrowth, including necessary tree reproduction, is eliminated by the hungry deer. They are constantly undernourished and may even starve in winter. Man then proves himself the enemy of both the deer herd and the forest.

Another harmful human activity is that of clearing the undergrowth under stands of mature trees. I know a small tract of woodland that was supposedly preserved for its primeval qualities. It was a fine remnant of virgin forest. But the agency assigned to protect it, in order to encourage public visitation, cleared out all undergrowth, instigated regular mowing, and developed a picnic area complete with tables, restrooms, and space for parking cars. Now the tract no longer sustains any tree reproduction, and a number of large trees have been killed from compaction of their roots by the admiring public. In short, it is no longer a treasured virgin forest—it is merely a park with scattered trees. Similar examples exist in many areas

The odd-looking saddleback caterpillar feeds on leaves of the redbud tree

of the eastern United States.

Man can also become an unintentional enemy of a forest when he tries to protect it from insect pests, especially alien types such as the gypsy moth. Wherever insecticides are used, they can be expected to kill more than just the target pest. They often wipe out beneficial insects and threaten birds and mammals that feed on them. The trend today, except in cases of extreme damage to large stands of valuable timber, is to try to avoid chemical sprays in forestland.

The logging of timber can be permanently damaging, and foresters are sometimes accused of being enemies of the very resource they are supposed to manage. Whether or not this is so really depends on the landowner's philosophy of harvesting. If all the best trees are cut first and the future is ignored, there will be nothing of value for a long, long time. But timberland owners and managers can no longer afford the wasteful frontier philosophy of "cut out and get out," for there are no new lands to exploit. Foresters should be accountable for the future potential of all lands they manage.

It is obviously true that a recently logged forest is no place of beauty and that for some years it may offer very little in recreation values. But it is equally true that if the soil is not damaged badly, if plenty of seed trees are left standing, and if the original diversity of life is not eliminated, the forest will restore itself. Proof of this is found in the wilderness status recently given to selected areas of our eastern national forests that once were logged; they are not virgin, but the scars of man are nearly gone.

The worst enemy of any forest is human activity that destroys the land's productivity. This does not mean the clearing of land for agriculture—unless it is clearly better suited for growing trees. Man often destroys the land in other ways.

Strip-mining of forestland without restoring the contour is certainly one way; not only is the mined area then ruined, but the acid mine wastes are permitted to spill upon surrounding lands and into streams.

Air pollution from mine smelting can be another way. An ugly example of this can be seen in extreme southeastern Tennessee, in the Copper Basin mining area. There, many years ago, sulphur dioxide fumes poisoned nearly 100 square miles of good southern Appalachian forestland. The result is a man-made desert of bare, eroded gullies that even today have defied human attempts at revegetation; the gullies continue to grow.

Each year large areas of deciduous forestland are being taken from production of trees by housing subdivisions, shopping centers, parking lots, highways—in other words, by the sprawl of expanding population in our industrial society. Such progress may one day threaten our future by destroying too much of the natural, productive lands upon which we all depend for food and wood, and a healthy, enjoyable landscape. In this way, as in no other, man's activities continue to be the greatest enemy of his forests. □

A HARVEST OF COLOR

Autumn is the time of harvest for farmers, gardeners, and many of nature's creatures. It promises a store of food for the long winter. But it also brings a soul-nourishing kind of harvest when deciduous forests dip into their paintpot of fall colors.

This harvest of beauty is an outstanding feature of most trees that drop their foliage for winter. The golden aspens of western mountains, in contrast to their background of somber evergreens, offer a good example. So do the deciduous forests of Europe. Yet nowhere do the intensity and variety of fall colors rival that found in our eastern states.

It is not a harvest that ripens overnight. The first tinges of autumn, like those of spring, are slow to develop. Late-summer woods, mostly devoid of wildflowers, now exhibit red and blue lobelias, orange jewelweeds, and modest bouquets of asters. But the foliage of trees on close inspection appears riddled by the work of insects. Their hordes dominate the forest at this season; especially at night their buzzings and raspings stifle other sounds and betray their frenzy to mate and lay eggs before the first frost. Spiders, though entirely silent, are also in evidence; the symmetry of their webs is everywhere, ready to trap a share of the insect hordes. Songbirds, meanwhile, gather strength for southward migration by gorging themselves on the spiders and insects.

The beginning of autumn is also a time for ripening seeds. All types have their means of dispersal—the exploding pod of jewelweed, the downy parachute of milkweed, the sticky chains of tick trefoil, the berries that pass undigested through birds' stomachs. Nuts and acorns seem to have no built-in means of dispersal. But there are squirrels to carry the heavy seeds away from parent trees, to bury them, and often not to return for their prizes; such are the nuts and acorns which grow into trees. In a forest the percentage of seeds that actually grow into plants is very small. Yet there is never any waste; seeds are food for wildlife—the tiny weed seed eaten by a sparrow, as well as the walnut that fattens a squirrel later fed upon by a hawk.

To the woodsman, early autumn is not the most popular of seasons; it is too late for the best fishing and too early for good hunting. Walking in the woods now brings a faceful of spider webs and clothing covered with prickly, clinging seeds. Yet it is only a pause, one that works to ripen the rich harvest of late autumn colors.

Days get noticeably shorter. Hot, humid nights of summer yield to a coolness that often leaves a shroud of fog in early-morning woods. Then there are the autumn rains; they prompt a ripening of late-season fungi, such as puffballs and coral mushrooms, and the white blossoming of that woodland wildflower which has no chlorophyll, the Indian-pipe. Soon nature begins to dabble on a palette of woodbine and sumac.

Then the first colors begin to show up on trees. Walnut leaves, the earliest to fall, show a hint of yellow before turning brown. They are followed by brighter yellows: those of basswood, beech, mulberry, tulip poplar, and the hickories. Finally come the brilliant reds and purples of dogwood, ashes, maples, sweetgum, and last of all, the oaks. Not all of these trees color the same woods; America's deciduous for-

Woodbine, or Virginia creeper, shows its fall color earlier than the white oak on which it clings

ests vary in species composition from place to place and this is what makes them so fascinating.

Some autumns in a deciduous forest are not as colorful as others. Occasionally the leaves fade due to summer drought, turn dull brown, and fall with hardly a trace of bright colors. This uncertainty, like that of the weather, makes for stimulating conversation. For instance, it is commonly argued that the best fall displays occur only after a hard, early frost; this is not necessarily true.

To better understand what generates the bright colors of autumn, one needs to examine the chemistry of individual leaves. Each species has its own blend of inherently colorful substances. The most obvious are chlorophylls, those green pigments so important in the food-manufacturing process of photosynthesis. But they are not the only ones. Nearly all leaves have—in addition to several types of chlorophyll—a yellow pigment called xanthophyll plus one of pale orange known as carotene. Any green leaves can be analyzed for presence of these pigments by the technique of chromatography. This involves crushing the leaves in a special solvent that dissolves the pigments, then permitting the colors to separate on a type of paper that absorbs them in distinctive bands. The technique is easier than it sounds and can be done in any high-school biology lab. By doing it a few times, one learns that if the pigments are not separated quickly after being extracted from leaves, the chlorophylls will deteriorate and lose their colors. Other pigments retain their colors longer; this helps explain why they show up so clearly in dying leaves.

As autumn days get shorter and nights cooler, the sap of trees begins to fall whether there is frost or not. Then a specialized group of cells at the base of each leaf stem, the abscission layer, hardens and seals off all flow of the life-sustaining sap. Each leaf dies and its chlorophylls rapidly deteriorate; this is when the xanthophyll and carotene pigments become unmasked. Yet all this accounts only for the yellows and pale oranges.

The brilliant reds and purples exhibited by dogwood, ashes, maples, sweetgum, and the oaks are due to an entirely different pigment known as anthocyanin. It develops in a mysterious way within dying leaves as a result of chemical breakdown involving trapped starches and sugars. The exact color of anthocyanin, like that of litmus paper used by chemists, varies with conditions of the leaf sap. It tends to appear red when leaf sap is acid, and bluish to purple under

Seeds of coralberry, sometimes known as "buckbrush"

Groundhog, or woodchuck, fattened for hibernation

Clouded sulphur butterfly on asters

Fallen leaves, mostly silver maple, on a woodland pond

alkaline conditions. This chameleon tendency is also known to occur in the color of certain flower petals as, for instance, garden-variety hydrangeas. It may explain why different trees of the same species can vary so much in the fall colors they exhibit.

Perhaps as varied as the blends on nature's palette is the weather that serves to brush autumn colors on the trees. Late-summer drought can prevent their being painted at all, leaving an entire forest dull brown; on the other hand, abundant rainfall is no guarantee of a colorful display. Hard, driving rain accompanied by strong wind may strip off foliage that is just reaching its peak of brilliance. The loveliest autumns occur when gentle rains are followed by long spells of Indian summer. This implies warm, sunny days and cool nights, though not necessarily freezing nights. A hard freeze will merely quicken the whole process of shedding and shorten the duration of peak colors.

The most memorable events in nature, as in all human experiences, are only too brief at best. It is so with the golden days of autumn. Peak colors are nearly over when the oaks, the last trees to be painted from nature's palette, begin to drop their leaves. Yet many of the oaks, for unknown reasons, hold tenaciously to their dead foliage; their dry, brown leaves may rattle on the branches throughout the winter.

But finally, when all the autumn leaves have fallen, deciduous trees are ready for the coming of spring. Wrapped tightly, minutely, in millions of buds are the complete embryos for new leaves and flowers. On a flowering dogwood tree, one can easily count how many blossoms there will be by the number of button-shaped flower buds. Anyone with good eyes or a magnifying glass can learn to identify all species of trees merely by their winter buds and twigs. They are distinctive in both color and shape; so are the abscission scars where autumn leaves broke off. The length of twig growth the previous year can also be noted, by closed rings of tiny scars where bud scales dropped off in the spring.

The fallen leaves, meanwhile, have their own special destiny and purpose. After blowing around for a while, or being lodged in the undergrowth, they are eventually packed down by rain and snow. The next spring they begin to decompose; fungi, insects, and countless other creatures of the forest floor render them back into the soil as undifferentiated humus. This will take about three years. Gradually the crop releases dissolved nutrients to be carried, through sap

Cardinal flower, a species common near streams, blooms early in the fall

Ripe berries of pokeweed in early autumn

Aster blossom with early morning dew

Leaves of flowering dogwood tree

from the roots, back into the treetops. The cycle is then nearly complete; it will make possible yet another autumn harvest of color. ☐

Buckeye butterfly, a species common in the early autumn

Banded garden spider on its web

THE HARDSHIPS OF WINTER

N o climate on earth suffers such extremes as that of the mid-latitude deciduous forest. At times it can be as hot and humid as an equatorial jungle; a few months later it can be as frigid and ice-bound as the arctic. The drastic change from summer to winter means hardships for all of its varied life forms.

To trees winter means the ultimate drought, for water that is locked into ice or snow is as useless to them as though it were nonexistent. To many warm-blooded animals it is the constant threat of starvation and freezing. Cold-blooded creatures can survive it only by the extended sleep—the temporary near-death—of hibernation. Yet it is the very fact that winter's perennial visit is as old as the hills—and likely older—that has made possible the necessary adaptations for surviving it.

All woody plants of the forest, whether trees, shrubs, or vines, make preparations during late summer. They do so by sealing the embryonic promise of next year's leaves and flowers within tightly wrapped buds. This accomplished, they are ready to retreat into dormancy.

The passing of autumn brings dormancy by causing most of the sap, though not all of it, to descend and to thicken. A residue of sugary sap does remain all winter in cell tubes of the inner bark and outer wood. It keeps the cells alive and maintains unbroken columns of fluid to help prime the pump of next spring's upward flow. Thus we find that live winter twigs, which tend to be green and supple, will break incompletely while dead twigs, brittle to the core, always snap in two easily. The residue of sap in a dormant woody stem, thanks to its high sugar content and viscosity, is kept from freezing and expanding and thus rupturing cell membranes.

By the time autumn's colorful leaves have faded and dropped, a deciduous tree has already placed its energy reserves into storage. This process was begun in midsummer. As the growing season waned, whatever sugar the leaves continued to manufacture was hauled downward, some of it to thicken the sap and the rest to be converted into starch for temporary storage.

Winter's loss of foliage by deciduous trees and other woody plants serves to prevent loss of moisture during the season when none is available. Bare branches are then free of leaves which would release moisture to the air and cause wind resistance; wind passes through branches easily with less chance of breaking or damaging them. Evidence of life in winter is betrayed only by suppleness of green twigs and the presence of well-formed buds.

Winter is an excellent time to learn tree identification, perhaps better than summer when leaves provide the easiest means. Close attention to bark, buds, leaf scars, and the branching of twigs will teach a person to recognize trees in any season. In fact, a worthy pastime for tree fanciers is to make collections of winter twigs and test each other in their identity.

While woody plants depend on latent buds to prepare them for spring, herbaceous types survive winter by more hidden means. The perennials die back to the ground and rely on rooted stores of sugar and starch for a resurgence of growth in the spring. And the annuals, inherently destined to live only one growing season, must produce viable seed to guarantee the next year's generation.

One of the pleasures of winter is the beauty of ice and snow

Only a few plants in the deciduous forest seem able to avoid winter dormancy. Certain mosses, a number of ferns, and an occasional broadleaved herb do remain green under snow and ice. None, however, can grow until their juices are aroused by the lengthening days of spring.

It seems a wonder, with so little greenery to sustain food chains, that animal life can survive the deciduous-forest winter. Yet that ancient, perennial tilt of the northern hemisphere away from a benevolent sun, and the eons of winters that result, have made possible the evolving of many remarkable adaptations.

Some creatures, those with great mobility, long ago adapted by learning to escape winter—they migrate. Most insect-eating birds, a few species of bats, and that remarkable butterfly known as the monarch go south, far beyond the horizons of their birth. Precisely how they read the celestial calendar that seems to trigger their migrations, and how they are projected along their ancestral routes—these are mysteries still unsolved.

The remaining forest animals have only two choices: to become as dormant as the trees through winter, or to actively survive in its harsh environment. By far the majority, in number of species, have no choice but dormancy. Included are all the types that are unable to maintain relatively high, constant body temperatures. In other words, the cold-blooded species.

By many ingenious adaptations, insects pass winter as eggs, pupae, or adults, hidden under bark, rocks, or within the upper layers of the forest soil. Reptiles tunnel below the level at which ground freezes. Snakes especially like to gather under rock ledges of south-facing slopes from which they can be awakened by a warming sun when spring returns. Frogs and salamanders burrow into the soft mud of their aquatic birthplaces. Fishes resting above them do not actually become dormant, but their activities and their appetites—as winter fishermen will attest—are somewhat less than they were in the warm months.

True hibernation among warm-blooded animals is not as common as some people tend to believe. A variety of forest mammals may sleep for several days at a time, curled up in their dens during the coldest weather, but this is not true dormancy. Even the black bear, known to sleep most of the winter, does not really qualify—simply because its body temperature and general metabolism do not drop appreciably below normal summer rates. There have been a number of

The purple finch is a frequent winter visitor to large areas of the eastern deciduous forest

Just how scarce food is in winter can be seen on this branch nibbled by a cottontail

The feathered remains of a minor woodland tragedy write a story in the snow: a hawk found itself a meal by pouncing on an unfortunate flicker

instances in which biologists visited the dens of wintering bears to study their sleeping habits and, in doing so, were suddenly and rudely chased out.

To be considered a true hibernator, a mammal must spend all winter in a constant, deep sleep with body temperature, heart rate, and breathing depressed far below normal. The only residents of the deciduous forest to qualify are the wood-chuck, the meadow jumping mouse, and most—though not all —species of bats. The eastern chipmunk, a creature that habitu-ally stores autumn food for winter meals, hardly qualifies except as an on-and-off sleeper.

Of all mammals that remain active through winter, the cottontail rabbit is surely the most vulnerable to hardships. It has no permanent den and has no instinct for hoarding food in autumn, and its usual diet of greenery is reduced to practi-cally nothing during the coldest months. In deep snow cotton-tails eat a scant diet of bark, often feeding at night, tracks telling their story in the morning.

Because cottontails lack the ability to turn white in winter, they are vulnerable to many predators. While serving as food for hawks, owls, and foxes, their numbers are continually low-ered. Yet the secret of their ultimate survival as a species is how they compensate in spring and summer by reproducing as only rabbits can.

Squirrels, though not as prolific as rabbits, also expose them-selves in the snow when digging through it for the mast of nuts and acorns they previously buried. But this mast, rich in both fat and protein, serves the squirrel better than the rabbit's emergency diet of winter bark ever can. Furthermore, the agile, tree-climbing bushytails are less vulnerable to certain predators. This comparison suggests how, as with all wild creatures, the normal breeding potential of a species tends to balance out against its expected mortality rate. Squirrels sim-ply do not need to reproduce as much as rabbits.

No winter food in the deciduous forest is as important as the mast from its trees. Deer and wild turkeys paw and scratch through snow for acorns. Bluejays and redheaded wood-peckers haul their share to hiding places among high limbs. The winter survival of many creatures, including even tiny white-footed mice which tunnel beneath snow, hinges upon the year's mast crop. It is either their salvation or, in a no-crop year, their death.

Small birds of the forest have their own special sources of winter food. Resident chickadees, titmice, and nuthatches glean insect eggs and other tidbits from crannies in the bark of tree

Though few scenes can compare with the beauty of a winter ice storm, it causes some of the most devastating hardships for wildlife. The ice can leave trees bowed and broken while crusting over the sources of food for animals of the forest

limbs. Woodpeckers pound diseased wood for dormant wood-borers. Juncos, finches, grosbeaks, and a variety of sparrows migrate down from the far north to seek berries and weed seeds along the forest edges. The larger ruffed grouse finds nourishment in a variety of buds.

Winter varies in the challenges it creates. Cold weather always demands abundant food to fuel the furred and feathered bodies of the forest; body temperatures must be properly maintained day and night. Deep snow obviously causes activities such as moving about and feeding to be more difficult than usual. In terms of hardships, however, no quirk of weather can quite compare with the damage wrought both plant and animal life by an ice storm.

It invariably begins with cold rain falling through an atmosphere whose temperature lingers near the point of freezing. As it continues, the twigs and branches of trees and the ground become sealed off in a crystalline overcoat. When the sun comes out again it may create a kaleidoscope of incredible beauty, but the result can be devastating. Soft-wooded trees such as elm, silver maple, and tulip poplar often suffer broken and splintered limbs. This leaves the torn, ragged edges of living tissue exposed to potentially invading fungi and insects. Old den trees collapse under the weight of accumulated ice.

An ice storm can cover animal foods with impervious, crusty coatings. Deer, turkeys, and squirrels can usually break through by pawing or clawing to get their share of fallen mast, but small birds have a difficult time getting to their needs. Under such conditions they die in untold numbers, either from slow starvation or the quick mercy of predators.

We might look upon the winter death of forest victims as a special tragedy of a particularly hard season, a situation to lament. This would be a humane viewpoint. But biologically, as with the rabbits mentioned earlier, there is no lament. Nature merely compensates. There is good evidence to show that when any species suffers considerable winter losses, its reproduction will actually be enhanced come spring. Stating it another way, ample spring populations do not breed as well as those below the environment's carrying capacity.

Perhaps we should view winter in the forest as a sort of biological purge to control populations. We cannot deny that the cycle of the forest seasons—with countless lives created and then taken away—does something for natural selection and keeps populations healthy. It is hardship with a continuing purpose. It is what makes life in the forest so diversified and maintains its dynamic balance. □

The ground squirrel lives on buried winter fare of fat and protein-filled nuts and acorns

RECREATION

The U.S. Forest Service often points out in its information leaflets that the areas under its management are "lands of many uses." This multiple-use concept should apply to all types of forest lands, private as well as publicly owned. Yet of all the many uses one might consider for a forest, none touch people more directly than those involving recreation.

To Americans living east of the prairie states, the deciduous forest is a convenient, familiar haven for escaping the demands of an industrial world. It is a place for enjoyment, beauty, and peace of mind. It attracts such varied activities as hunting and fishing, floating a woodland stream, family camping, nature study, orienteering, backpacking, and simply strolling among the trees. The more complicated our lives, the more eagerly we pursue such activities; they preserve our health, redirect our sense of values, and are treasured as part of our natural heritage.

Recreation is ideally a change in lifestyle, even if only for a few hours or a weekend. It is leisure with a purpose. It has grown with shorter working hours, longer paid vacations, more purchasing power, and increased mobility; it is the pursuit of happiness, American style. Sometimes, though, the quality of that pursuit falls short of the expectations of those people who are most anxious to find it.

There are urbanites who travel to the woods with the same trappings they sought to escape when they left the city on Friday evening. They look for campgrounds with all the conveniences—indoor plumbing and electricity—that they left behind. They find it difficult to tune out the television and tune in the woodlands. Such recreation, lacking any relief from the routine, can hardly be fully rewarding.

There are, of course, other people who travel in motorized campers only to use them as stepping-off places for real woodland adventures such as backpacking or running a wild stream. But even among these people who should know better, there always are a few who cannot enjoy the forest without spoiling the scenery; they leave trails of litter, hatchet-scarred trees, or the hazard of smoldering campfires. Their fault is not that of trying to take the city to the woods—theirs is simply bad manners in the outdoors.

It's therefore a fact that forest recreation encompasses as many problems as it does activities; like so many things we enjoy in the modern world, it requires both planning and management.

The kinds of recreation suitable for a particular forest depend on location, the size of the area, and the kind of ownership. An owner of a small woods, for instance, has neither the time nor the financial resources to invite public recreation; he reserves the privilege for his family and friends. A lumber company that owns sizable acreage might permit its use as a fringe benefit for employees, but private companies are not usually in the business of encouraging outsiders. Managers of public forestlands, however, must expect to oversee a variety of activities. As part of their recreation planning, they must assure protection of the scenery and at the same time satisfy public needs; their work is never easy.

A first responsibility of recreation planners is to rank potential activities according to their impact upon the forest and

Canoeing is rapidly gaining ground as one of the most popular woodland activities

upon each other. Use must be based upon a system of priorities. Thus a small tract of public woodland might be suitable for day hiking and picnicking but not for overnight camping. A popular area close to a large city might be fine for various nature pursuits but, due to the many people it attracts, could be unsafe for hunting. Backpacking and hunting are normally restricted to larger, wilder tracts of forestland.

If we rank the types of woodland activities from low-impact to high, among the lowest is nature study. Its most popular variations include identification, such as birdwatching, collecting, and photography. The collecting should not involve uprooting wild plants or removing rare or unusual animals. The taking of anything—other than leaves and invertebrates such as insects—often requires a special permit on public lands and usually is restricted to professional biologists. A popular piece of advice for anyone enjoying the woodlands is to take nothing away but pictures and to leave nothing but footprints.

Aside from the threat of too much collecting, there is another way that nature enthusiasts can cause harm: crowding the sanctuary of unusual life forms. This is precisely why some aged champion trees need a fence around them to protect their roots from trampling feet, and why federal law prohibits human visitation to the nesting sites of such endangered birds as the bald eagle.

One good aspect of nature study is that it is not—as a few people claim—frivolous. People well acquainted with birds, plants, and other forms are typically glad to share their knowledge without financial reward. As willing teachers they do a great service by planting the seeds of forest appreciation in the minds of others.

Another important kind of learning in the forest, one that is growing in popularity, is adventure and stress education. Participants are forced to learn basic survival skills by being placed in challenging, stressful situations. Activities are at first group-oriented; they teach members to share such experiences as sleeping in rain-soaked woods, rock climbing and rappelling, and taking part in exhausting hikes. Usually they end with a solo, which means spending a night alone in the woods without food or a tent. Such experiences are guaranteed to build a person's self-confidence and to create close relationships with fellow sufferers.

Still another form of educational recreation is orienteering. This involves racing through the woods, with map and compass as the only guides, over a predetermined course indicated by frequent checkpoints. Originated in Sweden, orienteering

Roadless areas are accessible to many recreationists. A camper lingers by his fire and lightweight tent…

…while an orienteering enthusiast confirms his position on the map. A compass will help him locate a hidden goal

has grown so popular in the U.S. that many areas have clubs devoted exclusively to its pursuit. Members strive individually to improve their skills by racing for the best times over courses of increasing difficulty. They can boast of knowing one of the purest forms of woodsmanship.

The impact of orienteering upon a forest tends to be negligible. If too many people run the same course, vegetation might be trampled; yet the idea is to avoid creating any visible trails. Adventure and stress-education courses can be more damaging, but only if too many groups use the same trails and campsites.

Although some people would disagree, the proper pursuit of hunting and fishing should have no greater impact upon the forest than the activities already described. This implies ruling out such slob behavior as violating game laws, cutting trees or fences, leaving littered campsites, and causing wildfires.

The true sportsman, well-trained in gun safety and well-versed in good outdoor manners, does not abuse his privilege; nor does the fisherman who takes pride in his particular sport. Antihunters may consider killing a harmful impact, but this is only a personal reaction and not in accord with unbiased biological principles. Natural deaths by predation are often more painful and slow than well-aimed shots, and are certainly far more common. Fish and game departments operate to preserve the renewable wildlife, not to wipe it out. They also try to ensure all the protection possible for rare and endangered species.

Hunters and fishermen as a group are sometimes criticized for a tendency to leave the highways and invade the woods in trucks and off-road vehicles, leaving ruts, erosion, and sloppy campsites. But any recreation group can and does attract its share of abusers. In fact, those who can be kept to the roads are easier to watch and control than those who might threaten the pristine fragility of restricted wild areas.

Trail-riding groups and their horses may have more impact upon a forest than a roundup of jeep campers restricted to a roadside. Too many hooves on a wilderness trail, and the waste they mash into it, can be a nuisance to hikers; grazing animals can reduce the wildflowers and other ground cover around choice campsites. But fortunately, managers of our public forestlands are fully aware of these problems; so are most of the wranglers who supply horses for trail-riding groups. They know they must exert proper controls over what is otherwise a worthwhile and very popular means of wilderness travel and enjoyment.

Although the individual is ultimately responsible, some activities tend to have more effect on the forest than others. Backpacking's increasing numbers have a major woodland impact

Bird photographers take a lot out of the forest—candid photographs—without disturbing the environment. As this blind attests, disturbance is the last thing the cameraman wants

Archer is the kind of hunter who allows his prey the most sporting chance. Man above uses a compound bow. Greasepaint smeared on hands and face complete woodland camouflage

This hunter goes after somewhat smaller game—creatures that dwell on the forest floor. His weapon is a magnifying glass. Nature study is a forest activity that causes little harm

Of all forest acivities, the one that may have the most far-reaching effects—bad and good—upon public lands is back-packing. There are two reasons for this; both reasons relate to a continuing growth in popularity.

Backpacking 50 years ago was a drudgery of carrying huge loads in clumsy, back-wrenching packs—hardly a pleasurable form of recreation. Today it has been vastly improved by the industries that provide us with contoured aluminum pack-frames, miniature stoves that boil water in five minutes, tents as light and compact as down sleeping bags, and just about any kind of food you like in precooked, dehydrated form. Back-packing has grown so popular that people seeking forest solitude may find, at least in choice areas, a scramble for crowded campsites. This makes it necessary for forest man-agers to require advance reservations from hikers who yearn for a true wilderness experience; it restricts the freedom of choice but is unavoidable.

Thus the first reason for claiming that backpacking has far-reaching impact is that it attracts too many feet to the most fragile segment of our public lands. People should not be al-lowed to crowd any forested area, particularly one preserved for its wilderness qualities.

The second reason is an outgrowth of the first. There is an ever-increasing demand for forestland suitable for backpacking. This clearly affects the priority system of management on public lands. Suitable areas must have some semblance of wilderness. They must be large enough to support miles of trails, well-spaced campsites near water, and no visible signs of commercial activity. Such requirements tend to generate strong conflicts of interest. Some recreation groups want a network of roads and campgrounds developed for vehicles—in other words, high-impact development. Lumber and mining companies often want no wilderness at all; their interests are totally incompatible, and they lobby politically against it.

It is sometimes argued that commercial use of forestland is in the best interests of the people because it creates jobs and salable, necessary wood products. This is certainly true with regard to private lands. But an attempt to apply this argument to public lands forces an unrealistic comparison between the dollar benefits of logging and of recreation. The commercial value of a timbered acre cannot truly be measured against its worth as a place for public enjoyment. Which are worth more, the thousand board-feet in a venerable oak or the footsteps of a thousand hikers who pass under it? Should wild deer and turkeys be assessed as part of the economy or as living symbols of our natural heritage? How do you compare industrial progress against peace of mind in the great outdoors?

Unless we can measure the pursuit of enjoyment in terms of dollars—as we can with board-feet of timber or tons of ore—conflicts with commercialism will always exist. The important fact is that public forestland belongs to the people and not to private enterprise. This does not entirely rule out logging and mining, but commercial uses should not have priority over demands of the public, which owns the land.

Forest recreation is many things to millions of people—all of them are important. The intangibles of beauty, wildness, and healthful outdoor pleasures need not be sacrificed in a race for more material goods and economic progress. Even the proud owner of a small woodlot knows that his personal enjoyment of the land, measured in footsteps, cannot be assessed in dollars. □

WE TAKE FROM THE FOREST

Our deciduous forestlands, if they were not so useful, might long ago have gone the way of our midwestern tallgrass prairies. That is, they would have yielded to the plow and nearly all become agricultural land. To be sure, much of the original forest has already been cleared for fields, cities, and highways; but for today and the future, we really need to maintain all of what remains.

Some forested areas are too rocky or steep ever to be cleared. If for no other reason, we need to protect such areas for wildlife and for their watershed value in holding back and gradually releasing the precipitation they receive. Much of today's forestland—especially that in public ownership—fulfills the vital needs of human recreation. And nearly all of it, both public and private, grows in importance because of what we take from it in natural resources.

No natural gifts are more renewable than those of a forest. Underground treasures of coal, petroleum, and natural gas will sooner or later be depleted, never to be renewed. Good topsoil, once eroded away, requires many centuries to rebuild itself. But the wildlife and trees of a forest, if managed on a basis of sustained yield, will continually replace themselves as long as humans exist to use them. Though our use of nonrenewable resources will surely be curtailed in the future, dependence on the renewables will never diminish.

All living forms in a forest, from the tiniest to the largest, are endowed by nature with more reproductive potential than the environment can support. Mice and rabbits must be controlled by predators. If deer become too numerous they will destroy the vegetation they need for food and many will starve. If too many sapling trees grow crowded in a clearing, competition will slowly but surely weed out most of them before they mature. Such are the ways of nature. Nevertheless, the environment tends to support as many of each species as an area's carrying capacity will allow.

If given the chance, every form of wildlife—deer, turkeys, squirrels, grouse, and all others either hunted or not hunted— occupies the forest at its own most favorable density. The same applies to trees, shrubs, and all lesser plants.

The turnover of animal lives is of course much more rapid than that of trees, but nature guarantees renewal in any case. Healthy individuals survive the sick; young replace the old. What foresters and biologists must do is to manage the resources for best use and enjoyment of the gifts they can provide, yet without endangering the environment or sacrificing the future. It requires careful, cooperative planning.

Unfortunately, though, more management problems are generated by people than by the forest's living resources. This is because nature's methods, even if predictable, cannot be manipulated to suit the personal desires of everyone.

For example, a real problem in managing wild deer is poaching—illegal hunting. In legal terms, wildlife in America belongs to all the people, regardless of who owns or manages the habitat. This means that poachers are really thieves; they steal from the rest of us and may even threaten the deer populations.

There are, on the other hand, people who oppose all hunting at any time. To fulfill their particular wish might result in overpopulation of the deer. This has actually happened in several states, partly because some of the original predators of

Quality white-oak log being cut or "bucked" from a felled tree. This deciduous species has a high market potential because of its many uses

deer—wolves and cougars—were exterminated from the deciduous forest, and partly because misguided people had too much influence in restricting the hunting regulations. Wildlife biologists do know how to manage deer herds but are not always permitted to act on their best judgment.

Foresters also find that human influences can be troublesome to the natural growth patterns of trees. There is a constant, ever-growing pressure for our forests to yield more wood products, even though Americans waste too much. One reason, obviously, is that the cutting of trees generates jobs as well as products, thus helping the economy. Another is the growing demands of an increasing world population—we export a large volume of wood. Yet the proper balance between sustained growth and harvest of trees is difficult to judge and is subject to various interpretations.

A forest composed largely of maturing trees does not produce the most wood in board-feet, but what it does grow is of high quality and thus much in demand. Clearcutting an area—logging off all its trees—will stimulate a large-volume growth of wood in countless young trees, but they will need to be thinned out, and no harvest of quality products will be possible for a long time. These examples suggest the continuing difference of opinion regarding two basic methods of managing and harvesting trees.

Even-aged management strives to grow trees that are all about the same age and can all be harvested at the same time when mature, by clearcutting. Uneven-aged management tries to maintain the deciduous forest as it develops naturally, as a blend of different species and age groups, to allow a partial and selective harvest at regular intervals.

Advantages of managing for clearcutting are largely those of economy for big logging operations. In that system, foresters do not need to mark each individual tree for cutting. Heavy logging equipment can be kept at one location until a patch is cleared; the larger the patch, the more economical the operation. There is less moving about, and the cleared areas, though they sometimes need replanting, enjoy a rapid regeneration of new growth. On any one location, the interval between harvests is long—at least 60 years—but companies that operate on large acreages can manage such lengthy rotations. They can also afford the expense of immediate replanting if necessary.

This method is especially practical with certain evergreens that tend to grow in pure, even-aged stands. Such trees as the Douglas-fir of the Northwest are intolerant of shade and need abundant sunlight for best growing conditions. Another

Another type of harvest taken from the forest is that of the sportsman. The camouflaged man shown above has been successful in a spring turkey hunt

advantage is that the evergreens, known as softwoods in the timber industry, are used mainly for lumber, plywood, and wood pulp; trees not large enough for the first two uses are suitable for the third. Thus all trees from a clearcut can be used and nothing need be wasted.

It is a different matter with deciduous trees. Many of them are somewhat tolerant of shade, at least in their seedling and sapling stages of growth. This is why they tend to grow in mixed stands of various species and age groups. Their wood is generally harder and has a different fibrous structure from that of evergreens; few are suitable for wood pulp. Finally, the vast majority of eastern deciduous woodlands are in relatively small ownerships.

Such owners do not have enough acreage to permit the long rotations of harvest demanded by uneven-aged management. In addition, they invariably value those forest qualities that provide benefits in beauty and recreation—the kinds of benefits not preserved by clearcutting.

Practically the only tracts of deciduous forestland large enough for rotations of clearcutting are on national forests. Much criticism of clearcutting has resulted from U.S Forest Service management on such lands. The most obvious mistake, often blamed on pressures from big logging companies, has been in allowing clearcuts that were much too large. This generated a number of objections. One was that such clearcuts ruined the scenic beauty of prime recreation areas. Another was that they caused visible erosion, the silting of woodland streams, and temporary damage to wildlife habitat. Those cuts also wasted the young, nonmarketable trees sacrificed in the act of clearing. Perhaps worst of all, clearcuts recalled stories and old photographs from generations before, depicting how early lumber barons destroyed our primeval forests. Rightly or wrongly, clearcutting has received bad publicity.

Fortunately, there are alternatives either to clearing large patches of forest or to the tedious practice of selecting a single tree for cutting here and there.

One of these is to practice even-aged management on a smaller, less visibly damaging scale. This simply means to limit the size of clearcuts to just a few acres. The other alternative is an improved variation on uneven-aged management known as the group-selection method. Though it requires careful planning by trained foresters, the method is especially adaptable for the owners of small to medium-size deciduous forests.

With the group-selection method, the forest is managed for harvesting in small plots of no more than one-half acre. Each

Walnut gatherers bring nuts to collection areas where they are fed through hulling machines. Hull fragments are valued as commercial abrasives

This deciduous forestland is being cleared for pasture. Though there is always a need for more good agricultural land, too many of our forests are being lost to farming, cities, and highways

plot is marked off according to its ability to yield two classes of trees: the first will be mature trees usable for quality wood products; the second will be crooked, damaged, or crowded trees usable for low-grade products or simply for firewood. This method can be economical for logging purposes if a number of the small plots in close proximity can be harvested at one time. Other plots in the same forest can be logged at intervals of 15 to 20 years, thus spreading out the income potential over an indefinite period.

Each harvested plot will allow ample sunlight for new trees that have limited tolerance to shade. This method permits good regeneration while at the same time improving the quality of the stand. Yet the mosaic of cut and uncut areas will not detract from beauty and recreational values of the forest, or cause damaging erosion. It will, in fact, preserve a diversity that is ideal for more types of wildlife.

In terms of wood products, a deciduous forest with a diversity of trees can offer more marketing potential than it would with only one or two species. As an example, buyers of wood for furniture need selected logs of various species, and the larger the better if they are seeking veneer quality. They depend mainly on owners of small, uneven-aged woodlands, not on operators of large tracts managed for clearcutting. This is an important point when considering that the vast majority of deciduous forests are in small ownerships.

Marketable uses for deciduous or hardwood trees are many, and some of them are quite specialized. Consider the black walnut. This tree yields one of the most versatile and by far the most valuable wood in the United States. It is not unusual to find old barns, built by original homesteaders, whose beams are sturdy walnut. But today the wood is much too valuable for use in construction. A few specimens of high quality are currently known to bring landowners as much as $10,000 when sold on the stump.

The best portions of a quality walnut, either sawed or sliced for veneer, are used for furniture. Small logs and even large branches are made into gunstocks or novelties such as bowls and picture frames; sizable stumps, if dug out by experienced handlers, may be sliced into exquisitely grained burly veneer.

Even the nuts are valuable. Extraction of the meats, rich in oils and proteins, from very hard shells is a specialized industry. But it doesn't stop there. The shell fragments, when reduced to proper sizes, are valued as abrasives in cleaning jet engines and automotive parts, in oil-well drilling muds, and as a filler for rough-textured paints. Such utilization is good conservation, making wise use of what might otherwise be waste.

Other deciduous trees have varied and specialized uses. Nothing compares with white oak for tight cooperage; that is, for staves to be made into leakproof barrels used in the wine and liquor industry. It and other oaks are also used as veneer for interior paneling or furniture and for hardwood flooring. Low-quality logs from the same species are usable for railroad ties, pallets, and mine props.

There was a time when certain hardwoods had only limited uses—for example: hickory for wagon parts and tool handles, ash for baseball bats. But wood utilization is a rapidly expanding technology.

Improved methods of seasoning freshly sawn logs by various kiln-drying techniques are allowing new uses for woods that would warp badly without such treatment. Lamination, or gluing layers of wood under pressure, permits the joining of attractive veneers to others that provide a strong backing. Even the cottonwood, long considered one of the cheapest of woods, is increasing in value for such uses. One product made from a variety of wood types is pallets. The demand for these slatted platforms, used in stacking factory goods and moving them around with forklifts, is growing constantly.

Thus, from the highest-quality logs to the lowest, our deciduous trees grow in value.

Wood products, along with watershed protection, wildlife habitat, recreation, and aesthetic beauty—all are valuable gifts from the forest. But they are best preserved by maintaining its diversity. A deciduous forest is a complex, living tapestry, woven with threads pulled together during countless centuries of evolutionary development. We cannot afford to tear apart its marvelous fabric. □

A FINAL PULSEBEAT

In 12 short chapters I have tried to show that a deciduous forest is not merely trees and their wood products, not simply a playground for outdoor pursuits, not only habitat for wildlife, not just a sanctuary for natural beauty. It is, or should be, all of these. A productive woodland is a complex tapestry of innumerable life forms, large and small, that have evolved to bring us many gifts. The more diversified it is, the better.

Contrast this with modern agricultural land. The pressures of expanding world population in our industrial society have locked us into a need to grow food by the monoculture system —that is, by cultivating a field for one crop at a time and trying to exclude all other life forms. Such a system, though apparently necessary to our economy, invites some costly problems: the need for various chemicals to destroy competing life forms, the loss of inherent fertility which must be replaced artificially, the demands of timely harvest and intensive cultivation for the next crop. Trying to grow trees by monoculture involves similar problems; much worse, however, it eliminates other woodland values that are so necessary to maintain the quality of our lives.

My home is surrounded by a small woodland that fills my leisure time with many interests and pleasures, but I am not really dependent upon it for my livelihood. In this way I am typical of the large number of citizens who happen to pride themselves in ownership of some three-fourths of all deciduous forestland in the U.S. There is no way that people like me could manage our limited acreages for the sole purpose of growing wood products. Even if this were possible, I doubt that many would want to do so; it would threaten to destroy more important values. Most private woodlands are treasured in ways that contribute very little toward making a living, even if they do occasionally supplement our incomes. They are more apt to be used for hunting, hiking, nature study, and such intangibles as providing solitude. They are maintained by the kind of stewardship that is a final thread holding together the complex fabric of their diversity. They are among the last private refuges from economic overkill and industrial blight.

This certainly cannot be said of intensively managed farmland. Nor is the final thread of stewardship guaranteed by corporations, which must judge their woodland assets in terms of potential profits for their shareholders. When a company's balance sheet indicates that wildlife habitat, recreation, and natural beauty cannot sustain its economic goals, we can expect these values to be sacrificed in favor of some attempt to grow trees like row crops, by monoculture.

Public ownership of woodlands is intended to safeguard the final thread; yet the quality of stewardship depends on certain variables. In parks, nature preserves, and wilderness areas a typical danger is that of overuse—too many people. They may leave trails of litter and damage native plants. This problem can be controlled by discreet methods of managing people. But where the public domain is open to commercial harvest of trees, or to mining activities, diversity may suffer unless it is defended by public opinion and the democratic process. For example, if large numbers of people do not mind clearcutting on recreation lands of our eastern national forests, they will certainly find it; timber interests will see to that. If enough people object, the Forest Service will be obliged to limit its contracts to selective cutting, which does not detract from aesthetic values.

The appropriate management of deciduous forestland is never an easy matter, even for the private owner. So many potential values are involved that a listing of priorities is worthy of careful thought. Because trees grow so slowly, and because we have the means to unravel the living fabric so quickly, management requires long-range planning and often professional help.

Our greatest problem, however, is not how to manage an existing woodland; the desire to do so, and to seek expert advice when needed, is obviously a step in the right direction. But how do we preserve remaining woodland from the onslaught of industrial progress? How do we save it from more highways, more subdivisions, more conversion to monoculture?

The answer, perhaps, is simply to enjoy and appreciate our woods of home so much that we cannot be tempted to sell out and lose its diversity of values. The quality of our lives—and of those who are to follow—depends on this. □

INFORMATION SOURCES

Selected References.   Due to the variations in scope, viewpoint, and information level of the following books, each one is provided with a brief descriptive comment.

Braun, E. Lucy. *Deciduous Forests of Eastern North America.* Macmillan. 1950.
   A detailed, authoritative description of forest communities in the eastern United States. It also tells something of their evolutionary origins; rather technical.

Collingwood, G. H., Warren Brush, and Devereux Butcher. *Knowing Your Trees.* The American Forestry Association. 1978.
   A practical guide describing 182 species of trees through photographs, detailed text, and range maps; primarily for identification.

Constantine, Albert Jr. *Know Your Woods.* Charles Scribner's Sons. 1975.
   Descriptions of various species of trees, with special emphasis on characteristics and specific uses of the wood.

Crockett, James U. *Trees.* Time-Life Encyclopedia of Gardening. Silver-Burdett. 1972.
   Attractive, well-illustrated volume on various species of trees, describing their special uses, site requirements, cultivation, and propagation.

Davis, Millard C. *The Near Woods.* Alfred Knopf. 1974.
   A naturalist describes his travels through a variety of deciduous forest types and tells of his observations in an easily readable style.

Farb, Peter. *Living Earth.* Harper. 1959.
   A detailed but highly readable account of the varied and numerous life forms that compose specialized communities in the soils under forests, grasslands, and even deserts.

Farb, Peter. *The Forest.* Time-Life Nature Library. Silver-Burdett. 1964.
   This attractive volume describes in text, photos, and maps some of the main characteristics of forestlands around the world; also provides a readable explanation of tree growth and physiology.

Forbes, Reginald D. *Woodlands for Profit and Pleasure.* The American Forestry Association. 1976.
   This is a layman's guide to the practical aspects of woodland ownership and management and covers such topics as silviculture, timber cruising and marketing, harvesting and selling wood, surveying, plus a simplified guide to tree identification.

Harlow, William M., Ellwood S. Harrar, and Fred M. White. *Textbook of Dendrology.* Sixth edition, 1979.
   A standard text for college courses in the study of trees, their names, habits, and principal botanical features. The description of each species includes black-and-white photos plus range maps; covers the entire United States.

Hylander, Clarence J. *Trees and Trails.* Macmillan. 1953.
   A rather elementary description of trees, how they live within a forest community, and a review of the major forest types in the United States.

Ketchum, Richard M. *The Secret Life of the Forest.* American Heritage Press. 1970.
   An elementary introduction to the major forest communities of the United States with descriptions of how trees are harvested.

McCormick, Jack. *The Life of the Forest.* Our Living World of Nature Series. McGraw-Hill. 1966.

An elementary exploration of the forest seasons and the various forest types of the United States; an appendix describes the National Forests and offers suggestions on preparing a terrarium and a collection of plant specimens.

Minckler, Leon S. *Woodland Ecology.* Syracuse University Press. 1975.

This practical book, aimed at the needs of small-woodland owners, covers the ecology, economics, recreation, and aesthetics of managing deciduous forestland in the eastern United States.

Neal, Ernest. *Woodland Ecology.* William Heinemann Ltd., London. 1958.

A small book describing how to conduct an ecological investigation of a woodland, based on actual field data from Thurlbear Wood, Somerset, England; written for students and their teachers.

Palmer, E. Laurence. *Fieldbook of Natural History.* McGraw-Hill. 1975.

The most comprehensive guide to the identification of typical plants and animals of all classification levels in the United States; also contains a section on astronomy and one on minerals.

Platt, Rutherford. *The Great American Forest.* Prentice-Hall. 1965.

Describes American forests of all types, their basic physiology, how they grow and renew themselves, and how man has altered their natural communities in various ways.

Platt, Rutherford. *The Woods of Time.* Dodd, Mead & Co. 1957.

Describes the world of plants in general; offers an interesting account of evolutionary events that brought about the development of today's deciduous forests.

Sargent, Charles Sprague. *Manual of the Trees of North America.* Dover. 1922.

A two-volume paperback set that describes the leaves, flowers, fruit, bark, and other characteristics of American trees.

Spurr, Stephen H., and Burton V. Barnes. *Forest Ecology.* John Wiley & Sons. 1980.

A technical, college-level textbook on all aspects of ecology relating to trees and forest environments.

Stoddard, Charles H. *Essentials of Forestry Practice.* Ronald Press. 1968.

Describes the basic, practical techniques of forestry for those interested in timber production; written primarily for beginning forestry students.

Field Identification Guides.   Many of these pack-size volumes are currently published in series form, with companion titles covering such varied natural groupings as algae, beetles, birds, fossils, reptiles, trees, wildflowers, and many others. The two series that are the most complete, attractive, and popular are:

Golden Field Guides, published in both paperback and hardback by Golden Press of New York.

Peterson Field Guides, published in hardback by Houghton Mifflin Company of Boston.

United States Federal Agencies. The following are important sources of information. Each one publishes a variety of pamphlets and bulletins relating to its particular jurisdiction.

Fish and Wildlife Service, Washington, DC 20240.

Has jurisdiction over wildlife resources on all federal lands, regulates the harvest and management of migratory birds and marine fisheries, and maintains national wildlife refuges.

Forest Service, P.O. Box 2417, Washington, DC 20013.

Has jurisdiction over all national forest lands and cooperates with state agencies in the management of wildlife resources thereon.

National Park Service, Interior Building, Washington, DC 20240.

Administers national parks, monuments, and other categories of federal lands classified as significant for their recreational, historical, or natural values.

State Conservation Agencies. This list includes only those having jurisdiction over forest resources in the states east of the Great Plains.

Alabama: Division of Forestry, 64 North Union Street, Montgomery 36130.

Arkansas: Arkansas Forestry Commission, Box 4523, Asher Station, 3821 W. Roosevelt Road, Little Rock 72214.

Connecticut: Department of Environmental Protection, State Office Building, 165 Capitol Avenue, Hartford 06115.

Delaware: State Forestry Department, Drawer D, Dover 19901.

Florida: Florida Forest Service, Collins Building, Tallahassee 32304.

Georgia: Georgia Forestry Commission, P.O. Box 819, Macon 31202.

Illinois: Department of Conservation, 605 Stratton Office Building, Springfield 62706.

Indiana: Division of Forestry, Department of Natural Resources, 608 State Office Building, Indianapolis 46204.

Iowa: State Conservation Commission, Wallace State Office Building, Des Moines 50319.

Kentucky: Division of Forestry, Capital Plaza Tower, Frankfort 40601.

Louisiana: Office of Forestry, P.O. Box 1628, Broadview Station, Baton Rouge 70821.

Maine: Bureau of Forestry, Maine State House, Augusta 04333.

Massachusetts: Division of Forests & Parks, Department of Environmental Management, 100 Cambridge Street, Boston 02202.

Michigan: Department of Natural Resources, Box 30028, Lansing 48909.

Minnesota: Division of Forestry, Department of Natural Resources, 300 Centennial Building, 658 Cedar Street, St. Paul 55155.

Mississippi: Forestry Commission, 908 Robert E. Lee Building, Jackson 39201.

Missouri: Department of Conservation, P.O. Box 180, Jefferson City 65102.

New Hampshire: Department of Resources and Economic Development, P.O. Box 856, Christian Mutual Building, Concord 03301.

New Jersey: Bureau of Forestry, P.O. Box 1390, Trenton 08625.

New York: Division of Lands and Forests, New York State Department of Environmental Conservation, 50 Wolf Road, Albany 12233.

North Carolina: Division of Forest Resources, P.O. Box 27687, Raleigh 27611.

Ohio: Division of Forestry and Reclamation, Fountain Square, Columbus 43224.

Oklahoma: Forestry Division, State Board of Agriculture, Capitol Building, Oklahoma City 73105.

Pennsylvania: Bureau of Forestry, Department of Environmental Resources, Fulton Building, Box 2063, Harrisburg 17120.

Rhode Island: Division of Forest Environment, Department of Environmental Management, 83 Park Street, Providence 02903.

South Carolina: State Commission of Forestry, Box 21707, Columbia 29221.

Tennessee: Division of Forestry, Department of Conservation, 2611 West End Avenue, Nashville 37203.

Texas: Texas Forest Service, College Station 77843.

Vermont: Department of Forests and Parks, Montpelier 05602.

Virginia: Virginia Division of Forestry, P.O. Box 3758, Charlottesville 22903.

West Virginia: Department of Natural Resources, 1800 Washington Street, East, Charleston 25305.

Wisconsin: Department of Natural Resources, Bureau of Forestry, P.O. Box 7921, Madison 53707.

Private Organizations.   All of the following have specific interests in deciduous forestland and its management.

American Forest Institute, 1619 Massachusetts Avenue, Washington, DC 20036.
   A nonprofit, apolitical, conservation-education organization supported by the nation's forest industries to encourage intensive forest management on commercial lands and promote the Tree Farm concept.

The American Forestry Association, 1319 Eighteenth Street, N.W., Washington, DC 20036.
   An independent, apolitical conservation organization dedicated to advancement of intelligent management and use of our forests, soil, water, wildlife, and other resources necessary for an environment of high quality and the well-being of all citizens.

Forest History Society, 109 Coral Street, Santa Cruz, CA 95060.
   A nonprofit educational institution whose purpose is to preserve the history of North America's forests, forestry, conservation, and wood-using industries.

Hardwood Research Council, 321 Parkway Building, Asheville, NC 28802.
   An organization of hardwood-using industries and others interested in research and education in hardwood forest management and utilization.

New England Forestry Foundation, One Court Street, Boston, MA 02108.
   A nonprofit organization for education in the management of private woodlands throughout New England, with emphasis on small ownership.

Society of American Foresters, 5400 Grosvenor Lane, Washington, DC 20014.
   An organization that represents all segments of the forestry profession in the United States.

Southern Forest Institute, 3395 Northeast Expressway, Suite 380, Atlanta, GA 30341.
   A nonprofit, apolitical organization supported by the forest-products industry in 13 southern states to encourage full development of the forest resource.

INDEX